Yamantaka

Lighting the Torch in the Three Blind Worlds of Buddhism

Ed Russo

ILLUMINATED PUBLICATIONS

BOOKS BY ED RUSSO

NOVELS

THE ILLUMINATI CODE: Mystery of The New World Order
THE ILLUMINATI CODE 2: The Apocalypse Begins
THE MERMAIDS CURSE
DEAD AND GONE
DIARY OF A MADMAN
LILAH
PLEIADIAN STAR CHILD
BLOOD TIES
SUMMER OF BLOOD
THE VAMPIRE BLOOD MOON
THE DARK LOVER
GOLDILOCKS 4017 and Beyond

NON FICTION
PLEIADIAN PAPERS
PLEIADIAN SPIRALS OF LIGHT: Workbook
THE HANDBOOK FOR THE RECENTLY DECEASED
LILITH: The Power of the Woman's Spirit in the Age of Aquarius
YOU ARE BUDDHA: Translation of the Vajarayana

An Illuminated Publications Book
Published by Illuminated Publications
ISBN 978-1-387-43454-1
1st Edition

Dedicated to all those who seek

Contents

INTRODUCTION

Many may wonder what or who is Yamantaka. Yamāntaka is a Sanskrit name that can be broken down into two primary elements: Yama, the name of the god of death; and antaka (making an end). Thus, Yamāntaka means "Destroyer of Death" or "Conqueror of Death".

Yamantaka, then, represents the goal of the Mahayana practitioner's journey to enlightenment, or the journey itself: in awakening, one adopts the practice of Yamāntaka, which is the practice of terminating death.

I will first talk about who Yama is. In Hindu Religion, Yama (Sanskrit: यम), is the lord of death. In the tenth book of the Rigveda, he is mentioned as one who helped humankind find a place to dwell, and gave every individual the power to tread any path to which he or she wants.

In East Asian and in Buddhist mythology, Yama (sometimes known as the King of Hell, King Yan or Yanluo) is a dharmapala (wrathful god) that is said to judge the dead and preside over the Narakas ("Hells" or "Purgatories") and the cycle of afterlife saṃsāra.

Although based on the god Yama of the Hindu Vedas, the Buddhist Yama has developed different myths and different functions from the Hindu deity. He has also spread far more widely and is known in every country where Buddhism is practiced, including China, Vietnam,

Korea, Japan, Bhutan, Mongolia, Thailand, Sri Lanka, Cambodia, Myanmar and Laos.

In Hindu lore, Yama was described as the first man who died that followed the path of enlightenment and was granted the position by the gods upon reaching heaven. In Tibetan lore, Yama was a monk that devoted himself fervently to Buddhist practice; on the day which would allow him enlightenment however, a criminal trespassed into the cave where he practiced and murdered him. Angered and with fury, Yama returned as a violent entity and slew his aggressor, but rampaged all across the land. The wrathful entity Yamantaka, or Daitoku-Myoo, halted him by showcasing a visage that instilled into him fear of death and that which he had inflicted on others; after this, he was allowed to judge the dead until the day when the cycle of Samsara would be ceased no more due to his merits and atrocities. Samsara is the cycle of death and rebirth to which life in the material world is bound.

There are ten worlds of Buddhism and three of them are the worlds of the blind which dwells within the subconscious. The practice of Vajrabhairava (rDo-rje 'jigs-byed).

In order to attain the state of Buddha we must get down to the subtlest level within us. The Yamantaka practice does just that.

Buddhism describes ten worlds which are ten conditions of life that we experience. It depends on our interaction in the world of which ne we move into any moment. We all have the potential to experience all of them, from desperate longing, self-hatred of Hell to the joy of Buddhahood.

The ten realms have been divided into six realms, followed by four higher states that lead to Buddhahood. The six lower realms are hell, hunger, animal, anger, humanity and heaven. Above these six are learning, realization, Bodhisattvas and Buddhahood.

Shining a light on the first three, instead of being at the mercy of our surroundings we can develop the ability to set our own direction and spend more of our lives being more optimistic.

Here are the ten worlds or ten realms.

Hell: A state of suffering and despair in which we perceive we have no freedom of action. It is characterized by the impulse to destroy ourselves and everything around us.

Hunger: The state of being controlled by insatiable desire for money, power, status etc. While desires are inherent in any of the Ten Worlds, in this state we are at the mercy of our cravings and cannot control them.

Animality: In this state, we are ruled by instinct with neither reason nor moral sense nor the ability to make long-range judgments. We operate by the law of the jungle and will not hesitate to take advantage of those weaker than ourselves and fawn on those who are stronger.

Anger: Here, awareness of ego emerges, but it is a selfish, greedy, distorted ego, determined to best others at all costs and seeing everything as a potential threat to itself. In this state we value only ourselves and tend to hold others in contempt.

Humanity (also called Tranquility): This is a flat, passive state of life, from which we can easily shift into the lower four worlds. While we may generally behave in a humane fashion in this state, we are highly vulnerable to strong external influences.

Heaven (or Rapture): This is a state of intense joy stemming, for example, from the fulfillment of some desire, a sense of physical well-being, or inner contentment. Though intense, the joy experienced in this state is short-lived and also vulnerable to external influences.

Learning: In this state, we seek the truth through studying the teachings or experience of others.

Realization: In this state we seek the truth not through others' teachings but through our own direct perception of the world. When we realize the impermanence of things then we no longer need to be a slave to our attachments. Happiness comes from realizing that you cannot control everything. We cannot hold onto anything because nothing is permanent. It is to truly understands the serenity prayer written by American theologian Reinhold Niebuhr (1892-1971), which is God, grant me the serenity to accept the things I cannot change,: Courage to change the things I can,: And wisdom to know the difference." Even though this was written by a Christian theologian, this prayer is the essence of Buddhism. That is to truly understand some things we have no control over, and that is all things change or die.

Bodhisattva: Bodhisattvas are those who aspire to achieve enlightenment and at the same time are equally determined to enable all other beings to do the same. Conscious of the bonds that link us to all others, in this state we realize that any happiness we alone enjoy is incomplete, and we devote ourselves to alleviating others' suffering. Those in this state find their greatest satisfaction in altruistic behavior.

Buddhahood: Buddhahood is a dynamic state that is difficult to describe. We can partially describe it as a state of perfect freedom, in which we are enlightened to the ultimate truth of life. It is characterized by infinite compassion and boundless wisdom. In this state, we can resolve harmoniously what appear from the standpoint of the nine worlds to be insoluble contradictions. A Buddhist sutra describes the attributes of the Buddha's life as a true self, perfect freedom from karmic bonds throughout eternity, a life purified of illusion, and absolute happiness.

Part One
Hell

Chapter 1
Samsara

Samsara is the cycle of death and rebirth to which life in the material world is bound. This is the level that goes on from lifetime to lifetime and will continue into Buddhahood. Samsara is due to our compulsiveness and confusion and disturbing emotions. Our karmic type of life is occurring on grosser levels, not this subtlest level that just provides the continuity. What we need to do is to somehow gain access to this subtlest level and not only stay with it, but work with it to transform it into the body, speech, and mind of a Buddha. In order to do that we must have a strong motivation, this is difficult when laziness, our own bad temper and anger, our own attachments prevent this.

This motivation is an enormous, tremendous compassion for everybody. The apathy that is fueled by laziness and unhealthy emotions is something we must cut through.

In order to overcome that confusion and laziness, we need the full understanding of reality - in Buddhist terms, voidness - that things don't exist in the impossible ways that our minds project. So with understanding, we want to cut through these grosser levels and get down to the subtlest level.

Normally we get down to that subtlest level when we die. During that period of death - what's called the clear light of death - before the bardo (the in-between state) and rebirth, we are just experiencing that clear-light level.

Usually when we experience death, we're totally unaware of what's going on - we don't recognize the potentials and abilities of that subtlest level of mind. We have all these habits of our confusion - all these habits of compulsive behavior based on confusion and disturbing emotions - and because of the momentum of so many lifetimes of being under the influence of these habits, what happens? New rebirth - samsaric rebirth - with another cluster of these habits being activated and generating the next samsaric life filled with the same types of impulsive behavior and confusion. This is our typical death cycle.

Going into the subconscious into the Three Blind Worlds we can then shed the light there and have an understanding of the human condition.

It is through the understanding of the human condition so that we can overcome that kind of death and through meditation, to get to that subtlest level of mental activity. This will allow you to have a clear light state in understanding of voidness or reality and how to use this understanding to transform into a Buddha.

Chapter 2
Yama as Judge of Souls

Unlike the god of the dead or the underworld in some other cultures, Yama is not always described as a punisher of the wicked. He is associated with wisdom and being very intelligent. The god is feared by some, though, especially because of his two great hounds. These fearsome creatures have four eyes and they guard the path which the dead must take to reach Yama. The dogs are sometimes sent to the world of the living in order to beckon souls to Yama. In other versions, a bird performs this duty, calling the dead to the god's city of Yamapura, deep in the murky underworld. In yet another version, Agni (the Hindu god of fire and son of Yama and Yami) leads the dead to Yama.

In one of the Upanishads, the Katha Upanishad, Yama is a teacher, which emphasizes his associated with wisdom. Later, Yamantaka becomes associated with Manjushri, who embodies wisdom or the understanding of reality. So already there's that association from Indian pre-Hindu culture in connection with Yama.

In Buddhism there are many protector gods that have been incorporated, and many of them come from earlier Indian non-Buddhist info. They are tamed and then given a pledge by Guru Rinpoche or others like him to protect practitioners. So they're brought into the Buddhist fold along with Yama. The different names of Yama in the protector practices such as Dharmaraja, Yamaraja ("King Yama") already existed prior Buddhism.

Yama is also called Kala. Kala in Sanskrit means "time" and "black" Kala means "time" because time is what brings death. The passage of time brings death. So another name for Yama is Kalarupa. Kalarupa, "the one with the form of kala" - which is time, time taking a form as the Lord of Death. You even get Mahakala associated here, which literally means the "great form of time." But what's interesting is the Tibetans translated kala here as black (nag-po), so Mahakala is called the Great Black One (Nag-po chen-po) in Tibetan. This is also where the name of the goddess Kali originates that is in the sanatana dharma which is known as Hinduism.

To be realistic, Buddhism didn't develop in a vacuum. Buddhism is an Indian religion, an Indian system, and it shares many things in common with Hinduism and Jainism. There's a general pan-Indic reservoir of ideas, concepts - things like Dharma, karma, rebirth, various deities, etc. all these different Indian traditions have their own variant of them, their own version. They are all talking about the same thing.

These traditions even traveled to Egypt and places in Europe, such as seen in Norse, Celtic and Etruscans and Sikel mythologies. The other cultures changed the names completely to fit their language. Much later the Italian and Sicilian myths of the witches came from the Etruscans, Sikels and Greek who was influence by the Egyptians.

So it's not surprising that you find all these so-called Hindu deities in the Buddhist practices. If you understand the way that ancient Indian society functioned, then you see that all of these people lived together, and so you have this common pool there. Then it becomes a little bit more understandable. All the various Indian deities, these various figures, are always riding on top of something. So Yama rides on a male water buffalo. You have Yama associated with a water buffalo. And he becomes a guardian of Hell. Within Hel are many hells.

The underworld is the subconscious and the Naraka (Hell) resides there. This place of torment is not an actual place like the Christian hell. It is a state of suffering within the mind. Of the Three Worlds of Buddhism, Hell is the first.

Hell: A state of suffering and despair in which we perceive we have no freedom of action. It is characterized by the impulse to destroy ourselves and everything around us.

Hell is created by the carnal mind and your higher Self, the Buddha mind will rescue you. Death is the separation from Universal Life. Hell is the torture from the passions of the lower mind, that longing, unsatisfiable hunger. I will talk more about hunger in part 2 of this book.

When we feel that our life sucks, and wish to escape it, that is the sorrows of hell encompassing us. Irrational thinking brings hell into our life. When we bomb other countries, we are creating hell, when we go against universal healthcare we are creating hell, when we are apathetic about people starving and homeless, we are

7

creating hell. It is the very systems that preach about being saved will save you from a literal afterlife hell that is actually creating hell in people's lives on earth.

The judging of Yama is not literally, it is the decisions you make. The Judge is your conscious. This is not a future event, this is happening now. Dead has nothing to do with physical bodies because people don't die, bodies die. The judging of the dead is the reactions of our mind based on decisions we make. The judgment isn't against people; it's against the things that hurt us. It is nirvana ("quenching.") So the great judgment flows down from consciousness by destroying that which ran your life amuck. Whatever regressive emotion you was addicted to is consumed.

Since all things are impermanent. Nothing stays the same, everything is constantly changing. When we are attached to things it creates anxiety because everything is fleeting. All things transform and become something else. The swirling red orange flames of pristine awareness of Yamantaka symbolize the catalyst for change. The flames burn away ignorance. When you allow the flame to burn away ignorance then you perceive it as the sacred fire that transforms you. On the other hand when you hold onto ignorance then you feel like you are being destroyed by the hot flames of Naraka or eaten alive,

Yama is sometimes called Dharma. This predates when Hinduism became codified, in the pre-Hindu tradition. Dharma in that tradition means "justice," justice in the sense of what maintains the order of karma in terms of rebirth. He's called Dharma, the Lord of Dharma, and

becomes Dharmaraja which means "King of Dharma."
Yama in Buddhism became protector after being tamed by
Yamantaka. There are three forms: Outer, Inner and
Secret Dharmaraja. Whatever we do when Dharma gives
us opportunity for enlightenment determines our karma.

Karma is not a force that reward's or punishes; it is that
every action has repercussions. A hot stove doesn't punish
us because we touch it; the hot stove just does what it
does.
Also every obstacle we face is not because of karma. Some
things just happen that are just opportunities for us to gain
skill and grow.
It is like a sport such as football (soccer). Your goal is to
make a touchdown. You have people who are trying to
tackle you, to prevent you from making that goal. Karma
has nothing to do with that, it is just part of the game. The
first time you might not make your goal. Instead of getting
upset, learn from it and build up your skill and eventually
you will make that touchdown.
This also apply in the game of life, challenges are just a
part of life that allows us to develop skill. Sometimes we
don't make that goal until we develop more skill.
It is up to us to take 100 % personal responsibility for
our actions or not. Our actions either bring us closer to life
or closer to death.

In life we attract what is needed for us in order to
learn. This is our Dharma. Sometimes we learn, sometimes
we don't, and it's all up to you. When circumstances come

9

our way, it's because that is what we need to learn from at that moment. When we sleep at night and have nightmares, it's because the nightmares are just a product of our own fears. In our waking life, the same principle applies. The nightmare that takes place in our waking lives is due to the reflection of our fears.

When there is a pattern in our lives that we don't like, we have to examine our self to see what it is about us that keeps attracting this into our life.

Those who take no responsibility will feel the flames of justice that is the pain and madness of their own making. Our actions are weighed and the universe tips that scale to what we do. The positive and negative are both weighed, the healthy actions versus the unhealthy ones. Whatever we have more of determines ones fate. This is our karmic repercussion. There is no being actually telling judging us and bringing a case against someone for their actions. It is all based on the scientific laws of cause and effect.

The universe doesn't care how good or bad a person is. It is indifferent. The universe is like a scale of balance that weighs our emotional tone. Happy cheerful thoughts are weighed on one scale. The unhappy, gloomy thoughts are weighed on the other scale. Whichever way the scale tips, that is what we will attract more into our life. If one focus a little more on gloom and doom thoughts than being optimistic, then more events to confirm to be sad about will manifest in one's life no matter how good a person is. The idea is to tip the scale in our favor by thinking more optimistic by having compassion toward our self and others.

Yama as the King of Hell is Pluto in Roman mythology which is Hades in Greek. Sometimes Hades is called Apollyon which in Hebrew is Abaddon which means Destroyer. It symbolizes old patterns that need to be eliminated if we are to grow and develop. Trying to ignore it will be havoc, physical and emotional upheaval. The cycle of samsara is the process of the cycle of letting go of old patterns until we reach Buddhahood.

Yama represents everything that is in your sub-conscious mind. Hell is not the imaginary place where wicked people go to be punished. It is like what William Blake describes, "So beautiful that it would agonize an angel to insanity." it symbolizes those things that you don't or can't understand. Also, it's from these hidden subterranean impulses of the mind that magical transformations originate. Yama is also called Dharmaraja which means Dharma King, the roman equivalent Pluto means riches. This is to mean within the subtle layers of the mind is a treasure. That gift is through Dharma and it's up to us what choices we make that determine our karma. When we are in harmony with Dharma then we grow towards enlightenment, we grow towards life that is our treasure. When we go against Dharma, it is like trying to stop a freight train with your hand. Therefore when challenges come our way, we must face them. What we are really facing when we face challenges is our self. Example would be that more than one person can face the same situation and it's only a challenge

11

to some and not others. In one scenario Tenzin walks into a room and sees a pile of money. He has no temptation to take it. He walks back out the room without touching the money. Next Passang walks into the room and sees the pile of money; he is very tempted to steal it. He walks closer to it and pauses. He then changes his mind and walks out without touching the money. Next Rinchen walks into the room and he is just as tempted as Passang, he walks over to it and decides to react by stealing the money.

Who experienced growth in this scenario? It was Passang. Tenzin wasn't tempted at all, so it wasn't his Dharma. That opportunity of Dharma was handed to Passang and Rinchen. Passang took this opportunity and faced his challenge and now closer to enlightenment. On the other hand Rinchen just brought bad karma toward himself for stealing the money. Is that bad karma punishment from an outside force? No it isn't, His actions and the seed he sowed in his mind acts as a ticking bomb that will put him in a situation to face an even harder challenge. It doesn't actually have to be shame that is the ticking time bomb; it is the impoverished thought that caused one to react in the first place. One has to think less of themselves to think they can only get that money by stealing because they believe they cannot achieve it on their own by legal means.

Wisdom is in the dark places within us, not outside us. Here is where you must see life as a game. I do not mean be reckless. Lasting power is when you face challenges in life. Many of us take life too serious and see challenges as problems. When we see adversity as problems it causes unnecessary stress. If you had this attitude while playing a game of baseball or poker, you would be tempted to quit when the odds appear to be against you. You continual playing because you see the game as a challenge which you find is fun. Therefore instead of seeing obstacles as problems, see them as challenges to overcome which are opportunities for growth. Many times we look outward to find the light. That is the wrong place, the right place is within.

In Peter Kingsley's book called In the Dark Places of Wisdom, he talks about how the ancient Greeks believed when the sun set, it entered the underworld where the source of lava is. The ancients then used this as symbolic that the light we seek isn't above, it's below, hidden within.

The book In the Dark Places of Wisdom and his book called Reality, is about that journey. To quote Margaret Starbird, the author of The Woman with the Alabaster Jar and The Feminine Face of Christianity said, "One of the most interesting books I've ever read is a book by Peter Kingsley called In the Dark Places of Wisdom. Wisdom wasn't just a matter of books. It was about going into the unconscious and minding the treasures of the unconscious through vision, dream, trance, and intuition; getting in touch with reality from within. And those are the kinds of secrets that we have lost in our whole western world."

In the East, they are aware of these secrets which are taught in Buddhism, Hinduism and Jainism. The dark places of wisdom are in the subtlest level within us.

Yama who rules these subtle levels within us becomes incorporated into the Shiva system of the Hindu gods. In Hinduism you have a whole group of deities around Shiva and then a whole group around Vishnu and Krishna. Another name for Shiva is Bhairava. So we get Vajrabhairava in the Buddhist variant, and they're basically just taking the name of Shiva and adding *Vajra* in front of it. Vajra means thunderbolt, which is the weapon of the god Indra.

In one of the Puranas, Shiva subdues Yama, and then Shiva is called Kalantaka, "the one who puts an end to kala." This means he puts an end to time which is another name for Yama. The Buddhist variant of Kalantaka is Yamantaka "the one that puts an end to Yama."

Chapter 3
The Forms of Yamantaka

Yamantaka is in the form of a very strong fierce figure and has Manjushri in his heart (very peaceful, calm, complete understanding of reality). This is, just in very general terms, a little bit of what is Yamantaka all about for those who might not have so much of a background.

In the Gelug tradition which is the newest of the schools of Tibetan Buddhism, this became very, very powerful practiced. In this system of putting together the three practices of these three deity systems - Guhyasamaja, Chakrasamvara, and Yamantaka or Vajrabhairava. Yamantaka is the container within which the other two practices can be included. And all the protector practices that are done in the Gelug tradition are all done within the context of oneself arising as Yamantaka.

Yamantaka practice became popular and widespread not only among the Tibetans, but also in the Mongol and Manchu regions in which Tibetan Buddhism spread.

Yamantaka is the name of a system of three sets of deities.

- Vajrabhairava

- Krishna Yamari (*that's Black Yamari, gShin-rje gshed nag-po*)

- Rakta Yamari (or Red Yamari, gShin-rje gshed dmar-po).

Yamantaka is the name for all three, but in the Gelug tradition the main thing that is practice is Vajrabhairava. Vajrabhairava is sometimes called just Yamantaka.

Vajrabhairava image is the one with the buffalo head and the Manjushri head above it. The Manjushri holds a sword in his right hand to symbolize cutting down ignorance. He appears in three basic forms. (In tantra every deity appears in so many different forms.) So we have:

- The one that is commonly practiced in the Gelug has nine heads, thirty-four arms, and sixteen legs. (Now, remember in tantra that having all these faces and arms and legs - they all represent different realizations, different aspects of the path that we want to be able to have fully realized simultaneously. By representing them by all the arms and legs and heads, it helps us to keep all of these things simultaneously in our consciousness. So it's a method.) This nine-headed form appears either in a forty-nine-deity mandala, a thirteen-deity mandala, or a single-deity mandala. (The mandala is the palace in which we live as this figure: not that there's a kitchen and a living room or anything like that, but we're in this palace. And the palace - every little feature of it represents some other aspect of the path and realization.)

- Then there's a six-headed, six-armed, six-legged version or variant, which is mentioned in the Chorus of Names of Manjushri ('Jam-dpal mtshanbrjod, Skt. Manjushri-namasamgiti). That's a Kalachakra text.

- And then there's a four-headed, eight-armed, four-legged variant, which is in the collection of jenangs (these subsequent permissions) called Rinjung Gyatsa (Rin-'byung brgya-rtsa, Source of Precious Means of Attainment of an Ocean of Yidam Buddha-Figures), a collection of about a hundred of these subsequent permissions. So there it's in this other form.

But all of these have a buffalo head and a Manjushri head on top. Black Yamari and Red Yamari don't have a buffalo head.

So what does this tell us? It tells us that there are many ways and many appearances of all these various Buddha-figures. And underlying it is what? It's the fact that a Buddha can appear in any form whatsoever in order to be able to benefit others. For some disciples, one type of form is more helpful; for other types of disciple, another form is helpful.[1]

The traditional account of how Buddha gave these teachings was that he arose in the form of Yamantaka. It was the same when Buddha gave the other tantras such as Guhyasamaja and Chakrasamvara, he arose in that form and gave the teachings. He gave these teachings in 100,000 chapters. This was preserved in the land of Oddiyana,

---

[1] https://studybuddhism.com/en/advanced-studies/vajrayana/tantra-advanced/what-is-vajrabhairava-yamantaka-practice

17

which is Urgyen in Tibetan where Guru Rinpoche came from. That was kept inside the Dharmaganja Stupa which was venerated by all the dakinis.

These teachings first spread from Urgyen to India in the tenth century by a great master from Nalanda Monastery called Lalitavajra, and then in the next century to Tibet. From Tibet it spread to Mongolia, and then the Manchus and it was a big practice in Beijing, where the Manchus ruled. This is what we hear from the Buddhist version of the history.

Remember when we talk about tantra and the accounts of how Buddha taught tantra not to think in terms of the historical Shakyamuni Buddha. That isn't the Buddha they are talking about. There is the historical Buddha and the allegorical Buddha. To not see this difference, then it will seem contradictory which can cause people to go to one extreme or the other arguing what is true or not.

In the Pali canon, Shakyamuni was a prince, and he had his life, and there are all these accounts of what he did during his actual historical life. That is one version that fits in with the Pali canon account of what a Buddha is.

The other is allegorical, in the Mahayana tradition Buddha manifests in so many different forms and in Buddha-fields, and he teaches to hundreds of thousands of devas and asuras and gandharvas incredible things. The reason why, a Buddha in the Mahayana tradition is one that teaches the entire universe.

The allegorical Buddha is someone who was enlightened many, many eons ago, who just manifests becoming enlightened, and who does these incredible things to teach the whole universe. Therefore if you take this literally and think the historical Buddha did that, then it can be very confusing.

Yama, Yamantaka and Urgyen

What is so special about Urgyen, the area where Guru Rinpoche comes from? That is because all the tantras come from there. In Buddhism it says that a Buddha will appear in a place where people are receptive, where it's most needed, and will teach in a way that the people of the time can understand.

That is a Buddha as understood in tantra. That's what a Buddha does. Urgyen was pretty much in the geographic center of a large empire called the Kushan Empire. Its dynasty ruled for a long time that whole area from Eastern Iran all the way over to north-central India, and so you had a mixture there of Iranian and ancient Indian ideas and mythology and various religious ideas, terminology, etc. We're talking about the period from the first to the early third centuries of the Common Era.

In this area you had the early worship of Shiva and the Shiva tantras and also Buddhism, so a mixture of the three. And they exchanged ideas. When you talk about different cultures being present in one area, they don't exist in isolation.

So these ideas about Yama are seeping in this area, with influence from these three different ways of thinking - the Iranian, the sanatana dharma, and the Buddhist. In the Buddhist variant, Yamantaka overcomes Yama - like Shiva overcame Yama using the name Kala, Kalantaka. And both Yama and Yamantaka have a buffalo head, a water buffalo head.

In the Buddhist story, a holy man who was told that if he meditated for the next fifty years, he would achieve enlightenment. This holy man meditated in a cave for forty-nine years, eleven months, and twenty-nine days - so he was one day short of the fifty years - and he was interrupted by two thieves who broke into his cave with a stolen water buffalo. First they beheaded the water buffalo in front of the hermit, and the hermit pleaded with them - "Please wait a few minutes more till I finish my fifty years of meditation" - but they beheaded him as well, before he could finish. After having his head cut off, this guy became so angry that he took the head of the buffalo that was cut off and put it on his own head and became Yama, the Lord of Death. He then killed the two thieves and drank their blood from cups made from their skulls.

And he was still so angry and upset; he decided to kill everybody in Tibet. So the people of Tibet were afraid for their lives, and they prayed to Manjushri to listen to them. And Manjushri transformed himself into Yamantaka, looking very similar to Yama but ten times more powerful and horrible, and Manjushri as Yamantaka then defeated Yama and made him into a protector for Buddhism.

In these mythologies, there are deeper psychological meanings within these myths.

In the first chapter I mentioned that when we die, the level of our mental activity that one has is the subtlest clear-light level, which is the clear light of death. Therefore in tantra we imitate death in meditation by using methods to get down to that subtlest level as well. So you imitate death and imitate the process of death without dying.

Yamantaka imitates Yama, both have a buffalo head. The practice of Yamantaka imitates the practice of death and what happens at death. That's why Yamantaka would also have a buffalo head just like death. This is how Yamantaka conquers death. It is through meditation that allows you to end samsara and reach immortality.

The Water Buffalo symbolizes Strength, Service, Dedication, and the Connection to the Earth Mother. This may be why Yama wears the male head of the Water Buffalo.

The image of Yamantaka is also shown with many arms like that of Avalokiteśvara who symbolizes infinite Karuna (compassion). Yamantaka has a fierce appearance whereas Avalokiteśvara appearance is that of a peaceful woman with many arms. Yamantaka's terrifying appearance symbolizes eliminating delusions and deceptions. It is the delusions and deceptions that cause self-cherishing. Self-cherishing starts with us trying to protect an image and images are all fleeting, all impermanence. When we come to realize that there is no separate individualized existence and that we live in a holographic existence like a movie projection, then we can let go of attachments to impermanent things that we want to keep fixed. We all share one Self, and it is our own experiences that make each of us individuals, other than that we are all One. This doesn't mean that we should shun being an individual as many may mistaken, to the contrary one can embrace their uniqueness without being attached. Our memories that make us individuals are to be treasured, but they are tools that we use. We are not our tools; our tools can be used to walk the path toward Buddhahood.

Like Avalokiteśvara, Yamantaka is also compassion, that compassion is manifested as protector from purging self-cherishing.

Here is what Dr. Alexander Berzin of the Gelug tradition said as Yamantaka as protector:

"First Yamantaka already appears as a protector early in the development of Buddhist tantra. You have Yamantaka appearing in Guhyasamaja already. According to some scholars that's already by the fourth century. According to tradition, however, Buddha taught Guhyasamaja to King Indrabhuti of Ogyen, who ruled during the second half of eighth century. Remember Lalitavajra, the guy who found it there in Ogyen, he's the tenth century. Already in the fourth century you find Yamantaka.

In Guhyasamaja you have what's called a protection-wheel practice - you have this in Yamantaka and Hevajra as well, very strongly in Yamantaka - and this is a protected space in which you have protectors in all the directions. Psychologically it's very important, actually, because in order to feel safe - even in a group-therapy session or in any type of psychological session - you need to have a protected space in which you feel that no harm can come from the outside and you can relax. And so, similar to that, you always set up a protection space. It's done in so many of the tantra practices. You have a protection wheel, it's called. Psychologically very helpful. So Yamantaka is already one of the protectors on this wheel in Guhyasamaja as well as on this wheel in the Yamantaka and Hevajra practices. Plus in the palace itself of Guhyasamaja, you have four gateways, and Yamantaka is there in one of the gateways as a protector also. In Kalachakra as well, Yamantaka appears as the protector of one of the gateways of the body mandala, as well as one of the sixty protectors in the protection wheel. In all these instances, Yamantaka has three heads, six arms and two legs, and is in the Buddha-family of Vairochana. Already before you get the development of Yamantaka as a meditational deity that you actually visualize yourself in that form, already Yamantaka appears as a protector to chase away interference." [2]

Therefore to reap is to meditate daily as a way to renew the mind and let go of the old. When we are attached to that which is impermanent, we choice to identify with inevitable destruction, which is because we are reaped with the material identity. Therefore we either reap through renewing of the mind to rise to higher consciousness, or we get reaped by nature when we hold on to an image we identify with. Being reaped by nature is death.

There is a period of phase that happens during death. One goes into a period of dreamless sleep for days. This trance state is what the Tibetan Buddhist calls the First Bardo. During this time, some traditions say special verse while the person is in this state. These verses help them move on to be recycled or to be reborn with all memories attached. This trance state is very much like when one is unconscious under anesthesia. The individual in this state has no sense of time. They have no sense of anything. That is why when one is put to sleep during an operation all they remember is counting and immediately they wake up and the operation performed is instantly done. This is what the

[2] https://studybuddhism.com/en/advanced-studies/vajrayana/tantra-advanced/what-is-vajrabhairava-yamantaka-practice

patient experiences, but the truth is they were under for hours during the procedure. During this stage in death of what the Tibetan Buddhist call the First Bardo is this same stage of no experience. Those who died may just recall what happen before they died, then find themselves climbing out of layers of dreams and witness observing their own funeral.

Using tantra meditation techniques one can also go further than the clear light level. Through mediation we can reach the bardo which is the gap between the cycle of death and rebirth.

Contemplation and meditation on death and impermanence are regarded as very important in Buddhism for two reasons. One reason is by recognizing how precious life is, and how short it is, we can live life to the fullest. The second reason is by understanding the death process; we can remove the fear at the time of death and ensure a good rebirth.

The way we live our life and state of mind at death, directly influences how we our future lives. You take your state of mind with you. If you die with guilt and shame, you will take that with you. It will be your own hell of your making. Its just like when you go to sleep at night, your dreams reflect what state of mind you was in right before you went to sleep.

The aim for the practioner is to have no fear or regrets at the time of death.

People, who practice to the best of their abilities will die, will experience a state of great bliss, according to the teachings. The mediocre practitioner will die happily. Even the initial practitioner will have neither fear nor dread at the time of death. One should at least aim at achieving at least the smallest of these results.

We actually experience bardos throughout our day. When you finish reading this session and look up, there will be a moment of bardo, it is that tiny gap following the end of one activity and preceding the start of another. If you notice them, these bardos of everyday life are places of potential transformation.

In meditation practice, you can notice the simple, nonconceptual awareness in the gap between thoughts. The bardo between death and rebirth is considered a particularly good opportunity for enlightenment.

Bardos are spaces that are of potential creativity and transformation; it is because they create breaks in our familiar routines. In that momentary space of freedom, the fresh perception of something new and awake may suddenly arise.

It is that pause, that stillness in every cycle. Toss a ball up in the air; it reaches its bardo right before it falls back down and at bardo when at rest. Energy at rest is the bardo seeking motion. Energy in motion seeks the bardo. Everything is the death and rebirth cycle. Within every cycle is the seed of the opposite, this is shown in the Chinese Taoist symbol of Yin/Yang. The Yin and Yang symbol has a white dot on the black yin side and a black dot on the white yang side. The opposite seems to contradict, but actually are complementary.

The bardo expressed as the pause in everything could be a millisecond or faster or slower. You cannot have motion without rest, cannot have one without the other. Without the inbetween, there is nothing.

I will use a lever and fulcrum as example. A lever cannot move without the fulcrum that represents rest. To quote the philosopher Walter Russell, "The Light of Mind is the zero fulcrum of the wave lever from which motion is projected. Its zero condition is eternal." Therefore everything returns to itself, like the serpent eating its tail or the circle. Another example I will use is the sun. As the gases that make up the sun expand, it comes in contact with cold space. It is in motion, once it's in contact with cold space the gases are at rest as the cold space causes it move back inward. Cold causes contraction. Contraction causes friction. Friction causes heat. Again the contraction movement of the gases comes to a pause and the heat causes it to expand again. This is the cycle that is in all matter, it's what gives matter the appearance of form. It is the seed of the opposite in every cycle that keeps it going on infinitely. As energy expands it comes in contact with cold space and then as it cools the friction causes heat.

When it comes to the seasons, it's the same. on the first day of winter, the sun is at rest in the southern hemisphere. Throughout the winter, the sun is gradually rising back up toward the northern hemisphere where spring and summer resides. Winter is the time of darkness, though the sun rising is symbolized as the light growing in darkness. The winter solstice tradition and Christmas that was chosen around that time is to remind us of that light. On the first day of summer the sun is at high noon and at rest right before it gradually descends back into the southern hemisphere where winter dwells.

Within us is the cycle of the seasons too. The winter is when we face challenges and spring and summer is when we Passover from winter into the spring in our lives. Some people may like winter better literally and allegorically. Being enlightened is to like and accept the complete cycle. Winter and summer will always come in our lives; the idea is to embrace both. Winter in our life symbolized by the underworld gives us opportunity for growth.

Those trapped in pipe dreams see the challenges in life that are problems that cause stress. The enlightened have fun facing challenges like when one plays a video game shooting an opponent. Those whose are not awaken will look at the challenges in life with contempt because they do not understand what is taken place.

We all go through challenges because it is the cycle of life. Some things happen to us due to our own actions and poor behaviors. Within the challenges is the bardo, this is when we take advantage of that pause and transform.

In chapter two in the example where the individual named Passang was tempted to steal the money, it was when he paused when he transformed. The bardo he experienced was when he stopped and changed his mind about stealing the money he was about to steal.

Death is a transition which is unavoidable in everything. Everything is transitory, nothing is permanent. For every death there is a rebirth. Everything changes. This is a cycle from when we are sent to kindergarten. Death to just being under our parents to birth of being around other peers in a class room. Death from elementary school from only having one teacher, to the birth of high school where we meet new students and have multiple new teachers. Graduating from high school is death from school to birth of being an adult. Every transition between death and rebirth is dwelling into unknown territory. For every beginning of any journey is the unknown. Use the bardo to change.

Change is unavoidable; you have to either accept it or feel the pain of non-acceptance. Many are too afraid of the unknown, so they rather stay where it feels safe, by holding onto temporality events and things. It is this refusing to accept that causes the making of our hells.

As said many times, hell is not a place, and Yama is not a conscious being. Yama is the dark evolutionary force of entropy that permeates all of nature and provides the drive for survival and propagation inherent in all living things.

It is the evolutionary force of entropy that is associated with the 2nd law of thermodynamics.

There is a misconception of the law of thermodynamics. Clausius originally wrote concerning the second law of thermodynamics is, "It is impossible for a self-acting machine to convey heat from one body to another at a higher temperature". This is incorrect because Nature is doing just that in every expression of gravity.

Every cold body of rain, or snow, heats as it falls to earth and brings that heat to lift the higher temperature of the earth to a still higher temperature.

"Every cold body which is added by gravity to a larger body at higher temperature raises the temperature of both bodies by the added crushing, compressing weight of gravity." --- Walter Russell.[3]

The misconception of the law was further explained by stating that an object will fall of its own accord from a higher to a lower level, but it will not rise of its own accord from a lower level to a higher level.

---

[3] From Walter Russell's book A New Concept of the Universe

This is also incorrect. "Everything which "falls" toward one of the two polarized conditions of matter must "rise" toward the other opposite condition. The interchange is equal." --- Russell

Only one side is seen, when it rains that water eventually goes back up as clouds. The apple that falls from a tree does the same. The water in the apple will evaporate and the decay will absorb into the earth as food for the roots of the tree. Meanwhile the apple seed will grow into another apple tree growing apples while the original tree will regrow the apple that decayed into nutrition.

This is not an objective universe, it's a cyclic universe. Objectivity is but one stage of a cycle which is forever moving through many stages between the appearance and disappearance of what the senses interpret as objective.

Yama would symbolize motion seeking rest, which is associated with the root chakra. Within the root chakra, Yama is a reservoir of power inside each human to be tapped at will.

Once we go inward and understand and embrace who we are, our perception changes. With self-acceptance, we love our self and love life. Hell is an internal state of unsatisfiable hunger. When we love life, we realize that any discomfort we experience is only temporary and like hunger goes away for a time when we take action. It's about realizing our Buddha nature. Yama is a symbol of Man living as what his animal nature dictates. Animals possess Buddha nature and Yama has the head of the water buffalo. Being grounded in reality one knows that death and pain is a continuing cycle in life, it cannot be escaped.

Knowing this, we learn to endure it and accept that it is part of nature. We realize this is reality and therefore to try to escape it as many do is foolish. Hell is caused by trying to escape reality.

Chapter 4
The Many Levels of Hell

Within the world of Hell, there are many hells. These are all different aspects within our self. It is the suffering that we experience and here is a myth of someone facing Yama and the divine messengers:

"Here, bhikkhus, someone engages in misconduct by body, speech, and mind. In consequence, with the breakup of the body, after death, he is reborn in the plane of misery, in a bad destination, in the lower world, in hell. There the wardens of hell grab him by both arms and show him to King Yama, saying: 'This person, your majesty, did not behave properly toward his mother and father; he did not behave properly toward ascetics and brahmins; and he did not honor the elders of the family. May your majesty inflict due punishment on him!'

(1) "Then King Yama questions, interrogates, and cross-examines him about the first divine messenger: 'Good man, didn't you see the first divine messenger that appeared among human beings?' And he replies: 'No, lord, I didn't see him.'

"Then King Yama says to him: 'But, good man, didn't you ever see among human beings a man or a woman, eighty, ninety or a hundred years of age, frail, bent like a roof bracket, crooked, wobbling as they go along leaning on a stick, ailing, youth gone, with broken teeth, with grey and scanty hair or bald, with wrinkled skin and blotched limbs?' And the man replies: 'Yes, lord, I have seen this.'

"Then King Yama says to him: 'Good man, didn't it occur to you, an intelligent and mature person: "I too am subject to old age, I am not exempt from old age. Let me now do good by body, speech, and mind"?' —'No, lord, I could not. I was heedless.'

"Then King Yama says: 'Through heedlessness, good man, you failed to do good by body, speech, or mind. Surely, they will treat you in a way that fits your heedlessness. That bad kamma of yours was not done by your mother or father, nor by your brother or sister, nor by your friends and companions, nor by your relatives and family members, nor by the deities, nor by ascetics and brahmins. Rather, you were the one who did that bad kamma, and you yourself will have to experience its result.' and so on for the other divine messengers: sickness, death.

"Then King Yama says: 'Through heedlessness, good man, you failed to do good by body, speech, or mind. Surely, they will treat you in a way that fits your heedlessness. That bad kamma of yours was not done by your mother or father, nor by your brother or sister, nor by your friends and companions, nor by your relatives and family members, nor by the deities, nor by ascetics and brahmins. Rather, you were the one who did that bad kamma, and you yourself will have to experience its result.'

"When, bhikkhus, King Yama has questioned, interrogated, and cross-examined him about the third divine messenger, he falls silent. Then the wardens of hell torture him with the fivefold transfixing. They drive a red-hot iron stake through one hand and another red-hot iron stake through the other hand; they drive a red-hot iron stake through one foot and another red-hot iron stake through the other foot; they drive a red-hot iron stake through the middle of his chest. There he feels painful, racking, piercing feelings, yet he does not die so long as that bad kamma is not exhausted.

"Next the wardens of hell throw him down and pare him with axes. There he feels painful, racking, piercing feelings, yet he does not die so long as that bad kamma is not exhausted. Next the wardens of hell turn him upside down and pare him with adzes.... Next the wardens of hell harness him to a chariot and drive him back and forth across ground that is burning, blazing, and glowing.... Next the wardens of hell make him climb up and down a great mound of coals that are burning, blazing, and glowing.... Next the wardens of hell turn him upside down and plunge him into a red-hot copper cauldron that is burning, blazing, and glowing. He is cooked there in a swirl of foam. And as he is being cooked there in a swirl of foam, he is swept now up, now down, and now across. There he feels painful, racking, piercing feelings, yet he does not die so long as that bad kamma is not exhausted.

The Narakas of Buddhism are closely related to diyu, the hell in Chinese mythology. A Naraka differs from the hell of Christianity in two respects: firstly, beings are not sent to Naraka as the result of a divine judgment or punishment; and secondly, the length of a being's stay in a Naraka is not eternal, though it is usually incomprehensibly long, from hundreds of millions to quintillions of years.

One is born into a Naraka as a direct result of his or her accumulated actions (karma) and resides there for a finite period of time until that karma has achieved its full result. After his or her karma is used up, he or she will be reborn in one of the higher worlds as the result of karma that had not yet ripened.

In the Devaduta Sutta, the Deva Messengers the 130th discourse of Majjhima Nikaya, the Buddha teaches about hell in vivid detail.

Narakas are thought of as a series of cavernous layers which extend below Jambudvīpa (the ordinary human world) into the earth. There are several schemes for enumerating these Narakas and describing their torments. The Abhidharma-kosa (*Treasure House of Higher Knowledge*) is the root text that describes the most common scheme, as the Eight Cold Narakas and Eight Hot Narakas.

Cold Narakas

The list of these hells are from Wikipedia on Naraka. [4]

- Arbuda (頞部陀), the "blister" Naraka, is a dark, frozen plain surrounded by icy mountains and continually swept by blizzards. Inhabitants of this world arise fully grown and abide lifelong naked

[4] https://en.wikipedia.org/wiki/Naraka_(Buddhism)

and alone, while the cold raises blisters upon their bodies. The length of life in this Naraka is said to be the time it would take to empty a barrel of sesame seeds if one only took out a single seed every hundred years.

- Nirarbuda (刺部陀), the "burst blister" Naraka, is even colder than Arbuda. There, the blisters burst open, leaving the beings' bodies covered with frozen blood and pus

- Aṭaṭa (頞听陀) is the "shivering" Naraka. There, beings shiver in the cold, making an aṭ-aṭ-aṭ sound with their mouths.[5]

- Hahava (臛臛婆;) is the "lamentation" Naraka. There, the beings lament in the cold, going haa, haa in pain.

- Huhuva (虎々婆), the "chattering teeth" Naraka, is where beings shiver as their teeth chatter, making the sound hu, hu.

- Utpala (嗢鉢羅) is the "blue lotus" Naraka. The intense cold there makes the skin turn blue like the colour of an utpala waterlily.

- Padma (鉢特摩), the "lotus" Naraka, has blizzards that crack open frozen skin, leaving one raw and bloody.

Mahāpadma (摩訶鉢特摩) is the "great lotus" Naraka. The entire body cracks into pieces and the internal organs are exposed to the cold, also cracking.

Each lifetime in these Narakas is twenty times the length of the one before it.

Hot Narakas

- Sañjīva, the "reviving" Naraka, has ground made of hot iron heated by an immense fire. Beings in this Naraka appear fully grown, already in a state of fear and misery. As soon as the being begins to fear being harmed by others, their fellows appear and attack each other with iron claws and hell guards appear and attack the being with fiery weapons. As soon as the being experiences an unconsciousness like death, they are suddenly restored to full health and the attacks begin again. Other tortures experienced in this Naraka include: having molten metal dropped upon them, being sliced into pieces, and suffering from the heat of the iron ground. Life in this Naraka is 1.62×10^{12} years long. It is said to be 1,000 yojanas beneath Jambudvīpa and 10,000 yojanas in each direction (a yojana being 7 miles, or 11 kilometres).

- Kālasūtra, the "black thread" Naraka, includes the torments of Sañjīva. In addition, black lines are drawn upon the body, which hell guards use as guides to cut the beings with fiery saws and sharp axes. Life in this Naraka is 1.296×10^{13} years long.

- Saṃghāta, the "crushing" Naraka, is surrounded by huge masses of rock that smash together and crush the beings to a bloody jelly. When the rocks move apart again, life is restored to the being and the process starts again. Life in this Naraka is 1.0368×10^{14} years long.

- Raurava, the "screaming" Naraka, is where beings run wildly about, looking for refuge from the burning ground.[5] When they find an apparent shelter, they are locked inside it as it blazes around them, while they scream inside. Life in this Naraka is 8.2944×10^{14} years long.[citation needed]

- Mahāraurava, the "great screaming" Naraka, is similar to Raurava. Punishment here is for people who maintain their own body by hurting others. In this hell, ruru[clarification needed] animals known as kravyāda torment them and eat their flesh. Life in this Naraka is 6.63552×10^{15} years long.[citation needed]

- Tapana is the "heating" Naraka, where hell guards impale beings on a fiery spear until flames issue from their noses and mouths. Life in this Naraka is 5.308416×10^{16} years long.[citation needed]

- Pratāpana, the "great heating" Naraka. The tortures here are similar to the Tapana Naraka, but the beings are pierced more bloodily with a trident.

37

Life in this Naraka is 4.2467328×10^{17} years long. It is also said to last for the length of half an antarakalpa.[citation needed]

- Avīci is the "uninterrupted" Naraka. Beings are roasted in an immense blazing oven with terrible suffering. Life in this Naraka is $3.39738624 \times 10^{18}$ years long. It is also said to last for the length of an antarakalpa.[citation needed]

Some sources describe five hundred or even hundreds of thousands of different Narakas.

The sufferings of the dwellers in Naraka often resemble those of the Pretas, and the two types of being are easily confused. The simplest distinction is that beings in Naraka are confined to their subterranean world, while the Pretas are free to move about.

There are also isolated and boundary hells called Pratyeka Narakas (Pali: Pacceka-niraya) and Lokantarikas. This literature contains 30 discrete scriptures in four groups (vargas). The fourth varga, which pertains to Buddhist cosmology, contains a "Chapter on Hell" In this text, the Buddha describes to the sangha each of the hells in great detail to the bhikṣus. The bhikṣus are male monks. the female monastics are called bhikkhuni (nuns). They are members of the Buddhist community. The lives of all Buddhist monastics are governed by a set of rules called the prātimokṣa or pātimokkha. Buddha describes it beginning with their physical location and names:

The Buddha told the bhikṣus, "There are 8,000 continents surrounding the four continents [on earth]. There is, moreover, a great sea surrounding those 8,000 continents. There is, moreover, a great diamond mountain range encircling that great sea. Beyond this great diamond mountain range is yet another great diamond mountain range. And between the two mountain ranges lies darkness. The sun and moon in the divine sky with their great power are unable to reach that [darkness] with their light. In [that space between the two diamond mountain ranges] there are eight major hells. Along with each major hell are sixteen smaller hells.

"The first major hell is called Thoughts. The second is called Black Rope. The third is called Crushing. The fourth is called Moaning. The fifth is called Great Moaning. The sixth is called Burning. The seventh is called Great Burning. The eighth is called Unremitting. The Hell of Thoughts contains sixteen smaller hells. The smaller hells are 500 square yojana in area. The first small hell is called Black Sand. The second hell is called Boiling Excrement. The third is called Five Hundred Nails. The fourth is called Hunger. The fifth is called Thirst. The sixth is called Single Copper Cauldron. The seventh is called Many Copper Cauldrons. The eighth is called Stone Pestle. The ninth is called Pus and Blood. The tenth is called Measuring Fire. The eleventh is called Ash River. The twelfth is called Iron Pellets. The thirteenth is called Axes and Hatchets. The fourteenth is called Jackals and Wolves. The fifteenth is called Sword Cuts. The sixteenth is called Cold and Ice.'"

Descriptions of the Narakas are a common subject in some forms of Buddhist commentary and popular literature as cautionary tales against the fate that befalls evildoers and an encouragement to virtue.

The Mahāyāna Sūtra of the bodhisattva Kṣitigarbha (Dìzàng or Jizō) vividly describes the sufferings in Naraka and explains how ordinary people can transfer merit in order to relieve the sufferings of the beings there.

Kṣitigarbha is a bodhisattva primarily revered in East Asian Buddhism and usually depicted as a Buddhist monk. His name may be translated as "Earth Treasury", "Earth Store", "Earth Matrix", or "Earth Womb". Ksitigarbha is known for his vow to take responsibility for the instruction of all beings in the six worlds between the death of Shakyamuni Buddha and the rise of Maitreya, as well as his vow not to achieve Buddhahood until all hells are emptied. He is therefore often regarded as the bodhisattva of hell-beings, as well as the guardian of children and patron deity of deceased children and aborted fetuses in Japanese culture, where he is known as Jizō or Ojizō-sama, as a protector of children.

Usually depicted as a monk with a halo around his shaved head, he carries a staff to force open the gates of hell and a wish-fulfilling jewel to light up the darkness.

Figure 1: Ksitigarbha

Figure 2: A mural from a temple in northern Thailand. The unclothed spirits of the dead are brought before <u>Yama</u> for judgement. Phra Malaya watches from above as beings are fried in a large oil cauldron.

Figure 3: Hell guards throw beings into a cauldron and fry them in oil.

These hells are symbolic of our suffering while living and what we take with us when we die. The Sutras of the Mahāyāna path shows us how we can chose not to suffer. The bodhisattva Ksitigarbha with his halo around his head and staff and jewel to open the gates of hell symbolizes the awareness to shine the light in the darkness of the blind worlds.

The hell of Thoughts is due to our own thoughts, Many times our own automatic thoughts get in the way which causes self-sabotaging. Many cannot understand why they just can't get ahead in life. They don't understand why they seem to always hit a brick wall. Many struggle with addictions and don't know why they cannot overcome them, no matter how hard they fight it. It seems to be an endless struggle with very little hope for many.

Our automatic thoughts cause us to react by flight or fight in a situation. Many times we don't even know why he run or react aggressively in certain situations. It is those reactive behaviors that usually self-sabotage us. The automatic thoughts are due to our own prejudices based upon our own personal experiences. When we are faced in a certain situation, the automatic thoughts that arise are because we are prejudging how the event will turn out based upon what happened in the past. On Bruce Lee's series Kung Fu, a shaolin monk called Master Kan said, "We do not punish for trust. If while building a house, a carpenter strikes a nail, it proved faulty by bending. Does the carpenter lose faith in all nails, and stop building the house?"

When our automatic thoughts react to a situation, we are no different than a carpenter who loses faith in all nails who decides to stop building a house. By understanding this, we don't have to let current situations hinder us because of something that happened in the past that we may or may not remember. Self-introspection is how we can learn to understand why we react the way we do it a situation. We then can be aware of a pattern in our life that may hinder us.

We all have goals and many times we are unaware of the pattern we have in our life that's in the way. We are all creatures of habit and many times our habits conflict with what we want. Many of our habits are due to reacting to our automatic thoughts.

Automatic thoughts are founded on inductive reasoning. There is deductive reasoning based on logic and there is inductive reasoning based on assumption.

Deductive reasoning is sometimes referred to as top-down logic. Its counterpart, inductive reasoning, is sometimes referred to as bottom-up logic. Deductive reasoning starts out with a general statement, or hypothesis, and examines the possibilities to reach a specific, logical conclusion. It is scientific thinking. It is also what most detectives use to gather facts during an investigation.

When we allow our automatic thoughts dictate us, fueled by emotionalism, such as our emotions control us, then we are no longer using deductive reasoning. Instead automatic thoughts take over which are based on inductive reasoning, inductive reasoning is the opposite of deductive reasoning. While deductive reasoning is used to reach a logical true conclusion, inductive reasoning is based on generalizing.

With inductive reasoning we make many observations, discern a pattern and then make a generalization. An example of inductive logic is, "The coin I pulled from the bag is a penny. That coin is a penny. A third coin from the bag is a penny. Therefore, all the coins in the bag are pennies." Even if this is true, inductive reasoning allows for the conclusion to be false. Here's an example: "Jim is a grandfather. Jim is bald. Therefore, all grandfathers are bald."

Many innocent people are in prison due to inductive reasoning. Inductive reasoning is the force behind conspiracy theories. It is this that also causes neurosis. In life situations it causes us to observe a pattern and then generalize. This is how people come up with the conclusion that all men are this way or all women are that way, or that since there is a pattern that things in one's life always goes wrong, and then it will always go wrong." It is these inductive thoughts that come from self-cherishing. Our thoughts fuel our emotions. Automatic thoughts are not based on reality, it is based on generalization. We must exercise our will to cut through those unhealthy emotions that are caused by our thoughts.

We are led to believe that we have free will. The fact is most of us are just reacting to our chemical stimuli and events in our lives. Most of our lives are just swayed by circumstances like a tree branch moving in the wind. We are addicted to the chemical stimuli that produce those feelings that are our comfort zone. This makes us a slave to our emotions. This means that we don't have free will. Free will must be earned. The only way to earn our will is to exercise our will. It must be exercised in order for our feelings to give birth to manifestation. An old Egyptian proverb says "Emotions are good servants but poor masters." Most of us allow our emotions to be our masters. The idea is to exercise the will so that our emotions can serve us in a healthy way.

When we exercise the will it impregnates the feelings associated with it. Newton's third law of motion is, "for every action there is an equal and opposite reaction." If you throw a basketball at a wall it will bounce back with equal force. The harder you throw it, the harder it bounces back. Emotions are like the basketball. Whatever feelings that you feed, the vibrations from those feelings project out and bounce back in the manifestation of circumstances. If we are stressed and focusing on what we don't want, those feelings will bring circumstance of that which we focus on that we don't want to manifest more. When we are slave to our emotions we are on autopilot. Those automatic thoughts bring feelings that are associated with our automatic thoughts. If we are not aware of those automatic thoughts we then feel emotions that are not pleasant and then we don't know why we feel that way.

To achieve a goal we must have desire. The desire must be empty, that means desire without attachments. The more clear the desire the faster you achieve your goal. Being clear is not having the fear of not having what we want. We live in a material world and it is designed so that we can grow through resistance. The resistance is challenges and opportunities for growth. Many people see the challenges as problems that they dread. They tend to let the challenges they see as problems that deter them from achieving their goals. One must realize that resistance is an opportunity and that is why we live in a material world. The material world is the whole creation and is the mirror of the Source that is Tathagata. Resistance is necessary for growth. The shell of a chicken egg which protects the embryo must at a certain time be destroyed or the chick

47

will be stifled and its further growth and development made impossible.

Another way to strengthen your will is to face your fears. Most fears that we have are toward things that are not harmful. There are rational fears and irrational fears. Rational fears are immediate dangers to avoid. On the other hand we need to face irrational fears. If you are afraid of rejection, face the challenge, rejection is not an immediate danger, it is just a response we interpret as personal that hurts our feelings. For any goal we must have courage to go for it. The unknown causes fright, to get anything done, is to face the fear and move through it.

For a week do something daily to face your irrational fears. First make a list, such as are you afraid to talk to someone? Are you afraid to ask your boss for a raise that you feel that you deserve? Write down those fears.

If you are afraid of losing someone who isn't healthy in your life at all, face the fear and depart from that person. You will feel better in the long run. Face those fears.

The second gate of hell is called Black Rope. This is symbolic of the black karma experienced by those who deliberately took actions to hurt others such as murder and theft. In this hell, they are made to climb hot black chains or ropes with heavy black weight packs on their backs while forced to climb flaming chains or ropes hanging over a fiery crevasse just to fall into painful torment and experiencing the same thing by climbing again over and over. This is symbolic of the suffering brought upon themselves through their own acts. This is a vicious cycle of a loop of suffering one experience internally. The punishment is symbolic of the way one's deeds in life metaphorically bind humans' soul to heavy weight of sin, where people have to carry sin with them forever in the repetition and repeating of the memories of these sinful deeds in one's mind without choice.

The symbolism of measuring the soul by using the black karma is used as a reference point about how the measure of black karma in one's life symbolizes the violence that one does to one's own psyche with each harmful act. There is also the idea of sin trapping people and confining then to motionless, helpless torture in lands were once comforting and comfortable to them, insinuating how sin dwells in the head, making one experiences a torturous Hell that takes place in their head.

There is also the concept of such violence acts against oneself and others manifest itself through binding people in ways where they are no longer connected to the land or their identities, losing sense of self and identity by performing such horrendous acts.

Each of these hells is allegories of what goes on inside our heads when we perform violent acts against our self and others. Each one is symbolically associated by the crimes we have done to our self or others, they symbolizes bad karma.

Chapter 5
The Nature of Suffering

Pain in life is inevitable though suffering is optional. Attachment to desire and ignorance is the cause of suffering. In Nichiren Buddhism, they have what is called the Three Poisons, which are ignorance, greed and anger. "Your practice of the Buddhist teachings will not relieve you of the sufferings of birth and death [Samsara] in the least unless you perceive the true nature of your life."[5] Ignorance is the number one reason for suffering. It is the ignorance to the nature of life. Greed, anger and ignorance feed of each other.

When we come into this world and observe it, we become convinced that we are separate from everything. We are caught in the illusion of separation. It is the concept of "I" and separate from everything else. This is the ego telling us, I am something unique and everything else is something different. It is this belief that gives rise to greed and anger. Greed is attachments, in other words it's an addiction. It is the ignorance of separation that causes us to fear and become overly attached to something. The masses believe that addiction only applies to substances. It applies to anything. It is actually the emotion associated with an object or concept that one is addicted or greedy for. That feeling we become greedy for can be associated with an

---

ideology, a drug, sex, food, people, romantic relationship, religion, money and so on and so on.

When we do not get our needs or wants met, then anger is triggered. When it comes to greed, our wants are never fulfilled and therefore it will always feed anger. Much of that anger can manifest as depression.

The belief that we are separate from everything also causes one too look outside themselves for validation. Ignorance gives rise to our perception of dualism. Greed and anger reinforces this view. It gives rise to the concept of I verses them. Guru Rinpoche said:

"From this identification stems the dualistic view, since once there is an "I," there are also "others." Up to here is "me." The rest is "they." As soon as this split is made, it creates two opposite ways of reaction: "This is nice, I want it!" and "This is not nice, I do not want it!" On the one hand there are those things that seem to threaten or undermine us. Maybe they will harm us or take away our identity. They are a danger to our security. Due to this way of thinking, aversion comes up... Then on the other hand there are those things that are so nice. We think, "I want them. I want them so much..." Through this way of thinking...attachment arises."

Ask yourself this, does space separate or connects things? The truth is space connects all things and they are only separated by language due to perception. This issue is that during our daily lives we only see one half of this dichotomy and not realize they are both two sides of the same coin. Dichotomy is in everything. Nature has dichotomies. That means everything has polarities. In Chinese philosophy, the yin and yang symbol describes how seemingly opposite forces that seem to contradict actually are complementary, interconnected in the natural world. In the image of the yin and yang symbol shows a white dot in the black half and the black dot in the white half. The dot expands becoming its opposite as an opposite dot appears in it. It is constantly moving. Within nature everything has both polarities and its labeled by which is the most dominant. The only difference between electricity and magnetism is both appear to move in opposite directions. This appearance makes electricity more dominant in the positive polarity while magnetism is more dominant in the negative polarity. Both contain positive and negative polarity and really is the same energy just appearing to be moving in opposite directions.

These opposites together are really Oneness. This Oneness is what the Chinese call Tao. Tao means the way. In Taoist metaphysics, distinctions between good and bad, along with other dichotomous moral judgments, are perceptual, they are not real. It's about perception and what is useful and what is useless.

What the Chinese call Tao, in Indian philosophies such as Hindu, Buddhism, Sikhism and Jainism it's called Dharma. In Buddhism, the word Dharma means "cosmic law and order." In Egyptian philosophy it's called Maat. Maat or Ma'at is the concept of truth, balance, order, harmony, law, morality, and justice. Ma'at has also been personified as a goddess to regulate the seasons, stars and the actions of mortals and gods. Ma'at is also symbolized by the balance scales of justice.

Due to this balance of polarities, nature has immutable laws. As I said earlier the Universe is neutral and indifference toward any concept of good and evil. That means there is no force or cosmic person that punishes us for our actions. You are either in harmony with immutable laws of nature or not.

Everything is made of energy; all space is filled with energy. It is just the different vibration that allows us to perceive certain patterns while other patterns are completely invisible to us such as space that connects all.

The I verses them, reinforces black and white thinking. Black and white thinking is thinking in absolutes, such as absolute good and evil.

All or Nothing, or 'Black and White' thinking is the thought pattern that allows us to generate a "flight or fight" response to danger. In this case one can't face reality, so he or she reacts to the flight or fight response and goes into survival mode and tries to escape reality by seeking external validation through greed.

Most life events are **NOT** 'completely disastrous' or 'absolutely wonderful' but contain elements of both good and bad. Depression makes people think in absolutes. All or

Nothing thinking is emotionally arousing, it causes over-dreaming and maintains depression.

Logical thinking is to learn how to tolerate uncertainty, there are no absolutes. All or Nothing thinking is the opposite of tolerating uncertainty. All or Nothing thinking is strongly linked with depression, and therefore we must think in shades of gray to tackle this issue. The more we polarize our thinking the more likely we are to become depressed because extreme either/or thinking stimulates the emotions much more. Oversimplify life and cause massive emotional swings.

This all or nothing thinking where the individual tends to think in extremes (i.e., an individual's actions and motivations are all good or all bad with no middle ground is also seen in the Abrahamic theistic religions. This is seen when others start wars or fights with others because they see believe they are right, therefore everyone else is wrong. To them wrong is evil, so they validate their actions because to them the other is evil and a threat. In the believer's eyes, the other has to change or be destroyed.

Anger and greed is also called aversion. Not only is it born out of ignorance, it reinforces our continuation of our delusion perception. This continuous cycle is seen on the image of the Tibetan Wheel of Samsara of the pig, rooster and snake feeding off each other (figure4). It is the Three Poisons of Ignorance, greed and anger that causes all of our suffering and unhappiness. As long as we act out of ignorance in trying to find happiness in a dualistic way, we reinforce greed and anger which causes more suffering.

When one focus on the concept that different things make each individual happy and that they have to find or pursue what makes them happy, they are missing the mark. All of those things they are mentioning are all external things. External things and events do not validate happiness, to think so is being caught up in the ignorance of the concept of duality. Happiness only comes from within.

Figure 4: Wheel of Samsara

Happiness does not come from outside us from events and things. All things are impermanence and therefore happiness comes from accepting that. To accept that we cannot control everything brings happiness. It is to realize that all is impermanence which means nothing is permanent and we have no control over that. Trying to make something permanent is refusing to accept reality. Since all is impermanence, then we are to have gratitude for what we do have and can change. Gratitude can do wonders and one lacks gratitude when they are busy focus on trying to desperately hold and change things that they cannot. Greed and anger reinforces the lack of gratitude.

When it comes to mantras, its isn't just in saying the chants and sutras, it is the manifestation of confidence, study and practice combined. One must have confidence in the internal Buddha nature. One must know that they have the potential within to attain Buddhahood. The mantras are to train the restless mind and embody the true nature of non-duality which exists in the bardo. Mantras shut down the automatic thoughts that are founded on prejudice. That prejudging that automatic thoughts do comes from the concept of duality. In the bardo which is the non-thinking state of rest, we can program our mind to anything we like, the bardo, the place of stillness is where transformation takes place.

The book Bardo Thodol which means Liberation Through Hearing During the Intermediate State also called the Tibetan Book of the Dead. This liberation from hearing is hearing the mantra during that state of silence, rest. With this, one can attain Buddhahood in this life time. Every individual has infinite potential, that means in each moment one has the power to change their future and influence the environment. In every moment is the bardo and in that stillness is a reservoir of unlimited potential.

The lay person believes that they are the character on the stage of life that is stuck in a role they believe was given to them. The enlightened one realizes they are not the character; instead they are the actor playing a role and have the power to rewrite the script to one's liking.

Everyone wants to be happy and many are ignorant of how to go about it, therefore when one seeks happiness outside oneself, one also sees that things outside themselves make them unhappy. This is what is behind the motive when one murders someone. In their delusion, one believes they will be happy once that person is gone who they believe is the source of their unhappiness. People murder for many reasons, it doesn't matter if it's for money, or to get away from abuse or an annoying neighbor, though at the core it's about happy verses removing what they thinks makes them unhappy.

When we get rid of duality thinking we are so unique from others, then we can understand and emphasize better with others. We can understand that we all want to be happy and just some are more ignorant than others on how to achieve that happiness. This removes the concept of judging others. No one can say if they were in the same situation as every individual that is in jail that we would have done something different if we were in their shoes, especially if we also lacked the knowledge in how to remove the concept of duality. All we can do is be grateful that we wasn't in their shoes and see that what happen to them, could have easily happened to us as well.

Also when we get rid of duality we see that we are interdependent. We realize that we are One. Oneness is not sameness, oneness is realizing how we are all connected as a whole, very much like how cells in the body all work together as a whole. All the cells are not the same; many have different functions though they all depend on each other. When the mantras are done in a meditative way, as though the manta is life itself which you are, it leads to realizing the oneness of all that permeates everything, yes everything.

When we see reality as it is, the concept of duality loses its grip on us. We are no longer seeing us versus them, no longer prejudging people or incidents and instead we see the oneness that causes us to appreciate things more which makes us happier individuals.

Part Two
Hunger

Chapter 6
Realm of the Hungry Ghosts

This is the second of the ten worlds of Buddhism. This is the second of the three blind worlds. That world is hunger. In another version of the myth when one dies they come face to face with the god Yama who is Dharma Yama holds in one hand white pebbles to symbolize your good deeds and in the other hand black pebbles to symbolize your bad deeds. The number of pebbles determines your fate. This is similar to in Egypt the goddess Maat has a scale of balance. Maat is cosmic justice. She weighs your heart which contains your good and bad deeds on one scale against the feather of truth. If you have more good deeds, your heart will be lighter than the feather. If your heart is heavier than the feather that means you have more bad deeds in the heart than good deeds. The weighing of the heart determines where one goes. In the Tibetan tradition if one has more black pebbles than white he may be sent to the realm of hungry ghost.

The eyes that see the description of the realm of the hungry ghosts are the eyes born of duality.

As a hungry ghost one's mouth is very small, the mouths and throats are the size of a pin with great big large stomachs. Because of this, the ghost can never get any food to satisfy their hunger. Their stomachs are always empty, for they can never get enough nourishment. They have an extreme need, extreme hunger beyond anything that you can conceive.

This hunger is symbolic of extreme neediness and longing.

As I said before that Yama is the dark evolutionary force of entropy that permeates all of nature and provides the drive for survival and propagation inherent in all living things. Because of this Yama is Dharma which provides each individual what they need in order to grow toward life. When people fight against it, they reap their own bad karma and then many refuse to take responsibility for their actions and cast blame on someone or an event or imaginary being. Rinchen who stole the money in the scenario in chapter 2 most likely refuse to take responsibility for his actions. He may blame the individual who left the money, saying the person shouldn't have left the money unsecured where anyway can get. He may blame the circumstance or cast blame on some imaginary Devil, blaming the Devil for setting him up for sending him there or blame the devil for tempting him. The devil, circumstance or individual who left the money had nothing to do with it. All this came from inside him. The inner source knowing what is needed for him to grow, allow the opportunity for Rinchen to grow and he didn't see it. The repercussions are all cause by himself. In myth Yama acts as a prosecutor. In reality we all have challenges which are opportunities to grow. Without growth, we become apathetic apathy brings death. When we become too lazy and apathetic, a challenge will come our way give us the opportunity to grow as a bodhisattva into Buddhahood which is part of survival.

By studying comparative religions, I notice the Satan in Jewish mysticism resembles Yama. The Satan of the Hebrews is not the Satan in Christianity and Islam. The Satan of Christianity and Islam is the epitome of evil. They believe in absolute good and evil. When it comes to the Satan in Judaism it does not represent absolute evil. Satan is neutral that means adversary. In Judaism and in the book of Job, Satan is the heavenly prosecutor and challenger. Everything he does to Job is all under God's orders. As prosecutor he is considered the Spirit of Wisdom who brings the record of your life before God in a case brought before you. Your fate is determined by that record. As adversary Satan is the temporary setbacks and challenges in our lives that are actual opportunities for growth. In Judaism Satan as adversary is also protector, sometimes the adversity we face in life protects us from walking into danger. In the story of Balaam, the seer who is asked by the Moabite king Balak to curse the Jews. When Balaam goes with Balak's emissaries, God places an angel in his path "l'satan lo" — as an adversary for him. In this story the angel God placed is called a Satan.

Satan is descriptor for individuals and situations that act as adversaries rather than a figure. The only times Satan is described as a figure is in the Book of Job and the Book of Zecharia where his role is that of an angel in divine court. Sometimes Satan is a metaphor for sinful impulses or Angel of Death. This is all symbolic of course.

The thing is as long as one doesn't take personal responsibility for their life, they will remain trapped in their hell.

Greed reinforces hunger. When we are attached to something, desperately trying to hold on to something, we lack acceptance and gratitude for what we do have. When a poor person is happy, it's because of gratitude. He or she is grateful for what they do have. When a poor or rich person is unhappy it is because they are not grateful for what they have.

Greed which is addictions causes an unsatisfiable hunger. One is greedy because no matter how much one gets what they want, they still long for more. Hunger drives our desires. What we all truly want is to love and to be loved. At the same time, part of our brain called the reptilian brain survives from the pleasure principle. When we falsely believe that we are the impulses of our drives, we give into them without any thought.

Jack Trimpey a California-licensed clinical social worker, the founder of Rational Recovery uses rational emotive behavior therapy, and cognitive behavioral therapy to overcome addictions. He uses a technique called Addictive Voice Recognition Technique (AVRT). This practice is of objectively recognizing any mental thoughts that support or suggest substance or any behaviors that we are ambivalent about as the AV (addictive voice). This AV comes from the impulses from the reptilian brain. This part of the brain controls our core survival functions such as hunger, sex, and bowel control. Hence, when the desires of this "voice" are not satisfied, the addict experiences anxiety, depression, irritability, restlessness, and anhedonia (inability to feel pleasure). Addictions are not just toward substances as many believe; it's toward any behavior that we are indecisive, about.

This includes those behaviors we just don't understand why we act on them that are against our better judgment. The step toward overcoming unwanted behaviors that lead toward grief is to objectively separate you from the impulses coming from the reptilian brain. When this part of the brain is unsatisfied it will convince you with your thoughts that it is you who want to act in this manner to avoid pain or seek pleasure. The key is to realize it isn't you that want to, it is the reptilian brain that wants to feel pleasure. Instead of saying to oneself, "I need, or I want. Use the technique AVRT and understand that "I don't need, I don't want, it wants a fix. You then don't have to act on it and can choose to give it pleasures in other ways. Giving it pleasures in other ways quiets the AV. Since we all want to be able to love and be loved our subconscious decisions are based on that. When one is incapable of loving themselves, they will seek to be loved outside themselves. If they cannot, many times one just does whatever one can to check out. They use something to distract themselves of not dealing with not getting the love they crave. Some will even go to the extreme and do something to get those 15 minutes of fame on the 6 o'clock news. All those subconscious decisions are based on wanting to be loved and when we are frustrated because our needs don't get met, we feel hurt and react in order to cope what we can't face.

As long as you stay blind to what's going on inside, you are subject to being a slave to your impulses.

Many who are in an anonymous recovery program may be familiar with the acronym HALT. It stands for Hungry, Anger, Lonely, and Tired. In the program it is said that this acronym is a danger in relapsing. Notice the first letter of the acronym is H for Hunger. There is hunger as far as not getting enough food and water as nutrients for the body. There is also the hunger that is due to attachments. It's okay to enjoy what you have to the fullest that is part of living. Though it's unwise to be so attach to something that you cannot see yourself living without it. Some things and the loss of love ones are very painful. That cannot be helped and grieving is a normal process. It is how we deal and perceive things that cause suffering or not. To feel that life cannot go on without them, is illogical and unhealthy way of viewing things. It causes one to go beyond the pain of experiencing loss. It causes long term suffering, even to those who take the easy way out through suicide. The individual who commits suicide to escape the pain, experiences in the afterlife what cause that pain in the first place that led to suicide. At that moment of suicide experience they will experience again the pain that lead to that act. They will experience it over and over again until they learned to change their perception. They will experience the same people they did when they was alive, it just won't be them, though in the mind of the experiencer, it will be them. The hells in Buddhism are symbolic of this eternal torment one carries with them while alive and in the afterlife.

There is part of the brain that survives on pleasure alone. It is the reptilian brain and it doesn't think nor care if it destroys the host which is you. It doesn't know that if the host dies, it dies too; it just survives on pleasure alone.

There are five basic needs that the reptilian brain survives from getting pleasure. It survives on pleasure and you cannot stop it, all you can do is to give it pleasure that is benefit to your well-being. Those five basic needs correspond to the five elements. They are:

The Five basic needs of pleasure
1. Fluids (water)
2. Food (earth)
3. Oxygen (air/wind)
4. Sex (fire)
5. Nurturing (Space)

The five basic needs are the world of hunger in Buddhism. It is in the realm of the chthonic, the subterranean aspect of the mind. In Greek myth it is Hades. In Hebrew it is call Sheol and in Sumerian it is called Irkalla, in English its Hell. In Tibetan Buddhism it's called Naraku.

When it lacks its needs in any of those areas, it manifest as cravings. The craving could manifest in the overindulging of one of the other or something totally outside those needs as a substitute. It is important to have these five basic needs fulfilled in some way. This is done through proper diet, exercise, meditation, having compassion to our self and others. When it come to sex, it can be with a social partner, through tantra or through transmutation. When it comes to nurturing, that is from compassion to our self and others and by socializing by connecting through a sangha (community). When it comes to transmutation, the sexual urges are not to be repressed. They are to be acknowledging while the sexual energy can be transformed into something else, such as creativity and enlightenment.

What is true happiness? As I said before, one must deal with reality as it is. The Buddhist see reality as voidness. This viodness or emptiness is that everything that we see or hear does not stand alone. Everything is an expression of one seamless, ever changing landscape. The universe is holographic and all apparent forms changes. Nothing is permanent and it's what the Vietnamese monk Thich Nhat Hanh calls "interbeing." When we realize this, then its irrational thinking to have towards things and people such as, "It must be this way" "I have to have this." That is not being objective, because things don't have to be a certain way. When you accept life is not a fix way and just because things don't go the way that you want it, doesn't mean it's the end of your world. Realizing this, then you can have true happiness, which is long term happiness. Long term healthy pleasure also adds to long term happiness. Buddhism isn't about short term hedonism.

Long term healthy pleasures comes from life fulfilling things such as long term pleasures that comes from long term investment in time, effort or money. It is having a rational self-interest by creating the life that you want which takes effort.

On the other hand short term hedonism causes unhappiness because these people are only concerned about the pleasure in the moment instead of the satisfaction and pleasure that comes from long term investment. These people who seek pleasure in the moment usually suffer from financial difficulties, health problems due to poor lifestyles caused by drugs, alcohol abuse and lack of exercise, and poor diet.

There are four reasons why people are compulsive about short term pleasures. Instant gratification, discomfort anxiety, entitlement and approval seeking.

Instant gratification: one feels that he must feel good right now. One doesn't have to feel good right now, if they do not, it's not the end of the world. By convincing ourselves that waiting is awful, then we just make things worst for ourselves. It won't be long before one starts sabotaging their goals through short term pleasures that will soon be replaced by shame and resentment.

The more you practice prolonging to have long term pleasure, the easier it will be. The more you give into short term pleasures, the more impulsive you become.

Discomfort anxiety: one feels that they shouldn't experience discomfort and that it should be avoided no matter what.

They feel discomfort and want to do something about it now. They think if they don't, then they won't be able to survive. Therefore they feel they need a drink now, or have to buy that new purse now.

These people fail to realize if they don't get what they want now, their lives will still be the same not a living hell like they imagine it will be if they don't get rid of their discomfort right now. Therefore instead of saying in jest, "I must not deny this pleasure now" say "I prefer not to deny this pleasure now, but I still will be OK if I do.

Entitlement: one feels that they are entitled to have what they want and when they want it.

Rewarding ourselves is a good thing, but when that so-called reward is in the way of your goals, and then it isn't a reward, instead it's a punishment. How many times you hear someone say something for example, "Yay the Steelers won, I need a drink" or "@#$ the Steelers lost, I need a drink." In the first example he is so-called rewarding himself because he is happy that the Steelers won the game, so he feels he is entitled to have that drink even if he cannot drink responsible and it gets in the way of his goals. In the second example he is angry that the Steelers lost, so he feels he is entitled to have a drink to get rid of his discomfort and also a way to punish himself because his team lost. In both cases, he is punishing himself if the drinking is sabotaging his goals.

At the core of entitlement is self-righteousness or self cherishing. Believing some people are better than others, so they feel they deserve a reward even when they aren't in discomfort. Many seek that instant pleasure just because they feel they deserve it because of what they went through that they believe makes them better than others. Self-cherishing is really low self-esteem where one has to elevate themselves above others to feel like someone.

By accepting that what anyone does doesn't make them special is the key. We are not our experiences; therefore no one is anything they do. Therefore it's about unconditional life acceptance. We are all equally worthy just because we are alive.

Approval seeking: believing our worth is based on what others think of us, so we try to do anything we can to win their approval.

Trying to get other people's approval is not going to boost up one's self worth. One thing is that you will never get the approval from everyone. While you may get approval from some, others will be turned away. Most of the time trying too hard to get approval from others backfires. Like I said thinking some people are better than others is just an illusion. Why sacrifice one's goals to just seek approval.

By giving up on our dreams to seek approval will detriment your life where it will make it even harder to retain the approval that you are so desperately seeking. It's just a waste of time.

Therefore be aware of what you may be doing that is sabotaging your goals. Many times it's our habits that are in conflict with our goals. We keep banging our heads at the wall, wondering why are we not closer to our goals, then give up with the saying in jest, "I guess it just wasn't meant to be". I think that is the biggest crap of an excuse that many people fall into. Therefore once you are aware what it is that you are compulsive about that is getting in the way of your goals, do what you can to start changing them. This takes conscious effort and doesn't happen overnight.

Taking care of the five basic needs reduces hunger. That is why diet, exercise, meditation and being part of a sangha is beneficial. The sangha is usually a Buddhist community. It can be any community that consists of like-minded people whose goals are similar to your own. Recovering drug addicts may choose anonymous meetings as their sanghu. It is up to each individual depending on their path of what they choose as their sangha.

Meditation helps us get our internal needs met, such as wanting to be loved. When we love our self unconditionally this is how we nurture our self. It is this compassion toward our self along with fulfilling the other needs to quench our hunger.

When we eat the wrong things, commit violent acts against our self it creates a longing that is like a bottomless pit that can never be satisfied. Neglecting our inner self by seeking validation outside our self, causes attachments.

The human being is not designed to do nothing; therefore we must balance things out as we live our life fully.

Chapter 7
Bardos

The word bardo means "an interval between two things." Bar means "interval" and "do" means two. It is the interval between the ending of one thing and the beginning of something else. The period between sunrise and sunset, the interval of daylight, is a bardo. The bardo can be a long or short duration. When energy as electricity spirals inward, there is a bardo before it spirals back out as magnetism. This period of rest in between is the bardo. The duration of the bardo determines the vibration frequency of energy. It is the frequency of this pattern that determines what we perceive in the objective world between forms. Everything that exist in the universe is different vibrations of the same energy and it all depends on the duration of the bardo in each cycle of vibration.

As I mentioned in previous chapters, our daily life, our experience is made up of intervals between one thing and another. There are a bardos between momentary thoughts that arises in us. As one thought fades and another thought arises, there is a bardo, even if it's an infinitesimal gap. It is a process that is within everything.

Within Tibetan Buddhism, there are six bardos. Each bardo are more important than the others.

1. **Natural bardo of this life:** The most pivotal is our waking life, from the moment we enter into this world till we die. This waking life is the first great

bardo in our experience. This is the "Bardo between Birth and Death' ('che shi bar do').

2. **Dream bardo:** The bardo of the dream level lasts from the moment we sleep at night till the time we wake up. This is the Dream Bardo ('mi lam bar do') which is that interval before we awake.

3. **Painful bardo of dying:** In an average individual, the trauma of death produces a state of unconsciousness, which can last a very brief time or much longer. It is said traditionally this period of blackout last three and a half days.

4. **Luminous bardo:** After that bardo, the consciousness of the individual begins to awaken as one climbs out of layers of dreams. That individual experiences things in a new way. This state of bardo from the trauma of death that leads to unconsciousness and then awakening in consciousness again is called 'chö nyi bardo.' The mind here is then plunged into its own nature, through a confused way due to ignorance.

5. **Karmic Bardo of Becoming:** The phase next after the death experience is the reawakening of conscious awareness which includes the many hallucinations and levels of dreams we experience after the after death state. This reawakening of consciousness is called the end of 'chö nyi bardo' to the moment we take actual physical rebirth in one of the six realms of samsara, known as 'si pa bardo', the 'Bardo of Becoming' or bardo of possibilities.

6. **Bardo of Gestation:** The sixth bardo is the 'Bardo of Gestation', 'che nay bar do'. Which is the interval

that begins at the end of 'Bardo of Becomig' as consciousness unites with sperm and egg in the womb that last till physical birth.

Meditation imitates this cycle of death and rebirth. When someone who begins to meditate effectively, there is a certain change in consciousness from meditation until they go back to worldly activities. The bardo of possibilities is in mediation like it is before one is reborn. When one is in that interval state of meditation in the silence, one can at that moment program the mind with any possibilities and come out of meditation to be anything we want. Instead of the slow process of the cycle of samsara, we can while we are alive, transform in this lifetime to become enlightened.

The Five Elements and the Nature of Mind

The unenlightened state of our mind is due to ignorance, this is called the fundamental discursive consciousness ('kun shi nam she'). It is this state that is confused and disillusioned. We can become clear where we no longer experience 'kun shi nam she'. We can instead experience wisdom consciousness ('kun shi yeshe'). The change in one syllable "nam: to "ye" can make that profound difference from fundamental ignorance to Primordial Awareness.

There are different states of consciousness within the mind that is associated with the five elements which are the essences with all of nature. It has these five elemental qualities, and it is from that potential that one experiences the death and after death states.

The mind has no limitation, it has no form, or geometrical position no more than space. Space has no limiting qualities; it's the same with the mind.

The mind is not simply empty; it has the illuminating potential to perceive anything whatsoever. This unlimited ability of mind to perceive is its illuminating nature, and corresponds to the element of fire.

This state of awareness is the highest state of awareness, the state of Nirvana.

Our mind which is unlimited and essentially empty gives rise to all experiences no matter what, is rooted in the mind like plants are rooted in the soil. Our mind rooted in experiences corresponds to the element earth.

The fact is that the mind can adapt itself to different situations. Through mediation we can transform our state of awareness; this corresponds to the element of water. Like water, it sustains its continuity and adapts itself to every contour as it flows; therefore the mind is also fluent, continuous, and adaptable.

From mediation our consciousness state rises. The mind is always moving as it quickly passes to another experience. It doesn't matter of one experiences pleasure or pain, or a sensory perception. The contents of the mind are always in a state of flux. This continual activity of mind is the element quality of wind (air).

The Five Elements in the Bardo

We are at a vital point between ignorant, unenlightened states of existence and the possibility of enlightenment.
Traditionally, the average person experiences the 'chö nyi' bardo which is the experience as a period of deep consciousness after one dies. This unconscious state is like being under anesthesia

The individual in this state has no sense of time. They have no sense of anything. That is why when one is put to sleep during an operation all they remember is counting and immediately they wake up and the operation performed is instantly done. This is what the patient experiences, but the truth is they were under for hours during the procedure. During this stage in death of what is called the bardo. Under this state of no mental activity, it's only a blank state of fundamental unconsciousness. The bardo ends as soon as there is a glimmer of awareness in the mind. In the interval between the end of this bardo and before the beginning of the next bardo arises what is called the 'Vision of the Five Lights'. These lights are connected to the five elements.

The different colors which the mind in the bardo state perceives are the natural expression, the radiance, of the fundamental, inherent, qualities of mind. The element of water is perceived as white light; space as blackblue; earth as yellow; fire as red; and wind (air) as green. These colors are simply the natural expression of the elemental qualities in the mind when the first glimmer of consciousness begins to appear.

As one becomes more conscious, they begin to perceive more, the experience of the elemental qualities also becomes more developed. What was formerly the simple impression of different rays or colors of light now begins to change into form. The light begins to integrate itself and balls of light in varying sizes begin to appear. It is within these spheres of concentrated light that we experience the 'Mandalas of the Peaceful and Wrathful Deities'.

In this context we speak of the five realms of existence in any one of which we may be reborn, because of the impure level of our experience. In the context of the five-fold mandala pattern, however, desire and avarice are combined, because they share the same basic nature of clinging. According to the Tibetans, it is this what determines what we come back as.

What matters the most is what you come back as after meditating.

The deities perceived are only projections of the mind, due to the concept of the "I" separate from everything else it's perceived as something outside us that can be overwhelming. After death experience, this can cause the mind to experience the Peaceful Deities emanating a brilliant light that the radiance can be overpowering like looking into the sun. The mind is then repelled by the experience and the confused mind is drawn to the samsaric rebirth. After the mandala of peaceful deities, then appears the 'Mandala of the Wrathful Deities. Again ignorance causes these to be something outside our self that is threatening.

At this point the after-death experience becomes terrifying and repellent, instead of an experience of the unity of the perceiver and what is perceived.

This overwhelming radiance that one has aversion to is due to hatred. Many carry around self-loathing and try to escape themselves thru being fixated on an image they identify themselves with. There is a difference between self-love and self-cherishing which is narcissism. Self-love is self-accepting all parts of yourself unconditionally. This means to accept all your strengths and all your weakness. Too many times religion or society projects an image of what we should be molded into. Many times its unrealistic and many won't accept themselves until they reach that image projected upon them.

Self-cherishing is not self-love, self-cherishing is actually self-loathing masked with an image.

A narcissistic individual doesn't accept themself. That individual is constantly fleeing from their self and hiding behind an image that they want everyone else to see. They are afraid to see themselves so they hide behind an image they wish they were.

This aversion is due to refusing to accept change which is part of nature, so we try to desperately cling to something we don't want to change. When we get eaten by anger, by hatred, we create our hell. Hatred is the most destructive of all emotions.

Enlightenment in the Bardo

The teachings in Tibetan known as the ' Bardo Tödrül and the empowerment connected is to help the practitioner develop an understanding and receive a blessing that will benefit them in the after death experience. When the forms are seen, they will understand that they are just projections from their own mind, hallucinations. Liberation is achieved when one realizes they are just expressions of the mind.

The teachings and empowerments connected with the Bardo Tödrül cycle introduce us to the deities and explanatory concepts and so prepare us for what happens after death.

The possibility of enlightenment in the after-death state rests upon three things. The first is the enlightened nature of mind, without which nothing would be possible. The second is the blessing inherent in what is projected. The third is the understanding of what is taking place.

The Bardos and Chakras

The chakras are associated with the six bardos. When it comes to death and rebirth process, it starts with the descending in the chakras. One descends as they experience the clear light into the sixth chakra, which is the Ajna chakra, this is the psychological center associated with awareness. The pineal gland sits here and when we meditate it releases melatonin and DMT. This is where we have our concept of our diety. The deity is a projection of our mind. When then descend to the fifth chakra, the vishuddha chakra. This psychological center is associated with speech and hearing. It is here where we encounter the peaceful deities and if we long to hold onto our ego, then we face the wrathful deities whose goal is to kill that ego you wish to hold onto. These deities are projections, hallucinations of the mind. Running from them is only running from yourself. When this chakra is open and balanced, you are able to express yourself clearly and honestly.

Here the truth of the mind is revealed. It is through hearing here in this bardo that leads to Liberation. We come to realize that we are not our words or thoughts. It is here where the judgment one used against the world is now turned toward yourself as discernment. Therefore instead of dissecting everyone else, that knife is now turned around to dissect yourself to see, what it is about you that needs to change. In Greek, this metaphor is called performing an autopsy on oneself. This is what is required to be reborn at a higher level.

The next chakra, the fourth chakra called Anahata chakra, this is the heart chakra. It is here where you chose to be released or not. It is here where decisions or choices are made. It is here where the god Yama symbolically judges your life. Your karma is determined by your actions. To fear Yama, is to fear the dark within, which means as long as you fear the dark within, you will always be at the mercy of it. The interlaced triangles symbolizes the neutral that links the higher chakras and lower chakras, it is up to use which direction we remain stuck in. This is the bardo of becoming and this hallucinatory state is said to last for a period of forty-nine days before the consciousness takes physical form again as an embryo.

Each and every being in the six realms of existence has what is called 'Tathagatagarbha', the 'Seed of Enlightenment', which is fundamental awareness of the ultimate nature of mind. Through this process by imitating death through meditation we make this transition here. Death is the ornament of life, death tries to break the ego. Breaking the ego means to break the ego grasping, where we no longer grasp the ego. The ego isn't going anywhere, therefore no need to grasp it. Yama is Death, Yamantaka is that which helps one overcome the fear of death while it destroys ignorance. Ignorance is to ignore the truth. The Wheel of Samsara of the pig, rooster and snake feeding off each other represents the three lower chakras. Those three animals symbolize ignorance (pig), lust (rooster) and malice (snake). The heart chakra is where you choose between your body as the vehicle you identify with or your light body. It is here what determines what you become or experience. In Egyptian Book of the Dead, there is an image of the crocodile Ammit biting below the heart chakra. This is symbolic of when the heart is weighed by the goddess Maat who would be Dharma or Yama. If the heart is light it would avoid the lower realm where Ammit is. Those whose heart is heaven, the heart is devoured by Ammit.

Through tantra we can take our vices and turn it around to benefit us. If you are passionate, don't feel bad, be passionate, and use your passionate behavior towards enlightenment.

The ḍākiṇīs are fire women from outer space and one for example called Vajrayoginī who holds a vajra in her right hand that symbolizes illumination. In her left hand she holds a bowl made of a top of a skull while she drinks blood, while she tramples on the mere animal nature. Vajrayoginī's essence is "great passion" (maharaga), a transcendent passion that is free of selfishness and illusion, and intensely works for the well-being of others and for the destruction of ego clinging.

After the bardo of becoming one descends to the second chakra called the swadisthana chakra or sacral chakra. It is here one sees many couples copulating. Meditate upon these visions. The visions of couples having sex means that you are about to have a new life. This symbology is the different states as we descend from the crown chakra to the root chakra. Here in the root, we must have a understanding before we can ascend back up. To try to ascend without any knowledge of the root chakra is like building a house on sand. That means any storm that comes in your life will knock that house down. To not have any knowledge of the root is due to ignoring our carnal nature which only makes us at their mercy when ignored. There is a saying in the west, the 'The greatest trick the Devil ever pulled was convincing the world he didn't exist." This phrase is means that if we ignore the dark in us because we are afraid and rather pretend it's not there, they will cause havoc in our life.

When we understand the human what causes hunger and understand our human animal nature then we can have compassion instead of avarice. To ignore what lives in the root chakra is fleeing from one self, which means there is fear and self-loathing. How can one truly love themselves if there are parts of themselves they refuse to acknowledge? One cannot.

One must have compassion towards all, including themselves. The vice of compassion is the attachment to what you love. Refusing to let go of what you love is not compassion. This only causes suffering to the one holding on. If what they are holding to is a person, then they are causing that one who wants to move on, unnecessary pain. Therefore we must have compassion which starts from accepting all expects of our self and transform our vices into virtues. Tantra isn't about getting rid of anger, lust etc, its about taking that and transforming it. If you are an angry person, don't repress it. Instead find out why you are angry and then use that energy to do something that you do have control over instead of being angry at stuff you cannot change.

I cannot change people who are ignorant, or how people use that ignorance to destroy themselves or others. Those things make me angry. All I can do is turn that around and write and teach those who are willing to learn as I use that energy to transform myself so that I can be the best me in order to help others. First we must understand why we have these vices to begin with.

Chapter 8
Shine the Light in Darkness, be Love, Show Compassion

The dark gods in myth are symbolic of the subterranean world within our mind. Those names could be called by many names, Yama, Hecate, Abaddon, Apollyon, Hades, Irkalla and many others. Other than Hecate and Yama, all these names listed here are names of gods and the places they dwell. This is symbolic of the subconscious.

The five basic needs are the world of hunger in Buddhism. As I said earlier in the book they are fluids, food, oxygen, sex and nurturing. It is in the realm of the chthonic, the subterranean aspect of the mind. In Greek myth it is Hades. In Hebrew it is call Sheol and in Sumerian it is called Irkalla, in English its Hell. The hunger leads to addiction when we are lacking pleasure in one of those areas.

The more one is attached to something, the more pain and threat one feels towards its loss. The more pain and threat, the more desperate measures one takes to prevent loss. Human selfishness and addiction is the core of all evil. That selfishness is ignorance and addiction is greed.

All addictions are emotionalism. The things we become addicted to isn't the object of our desire, it's the feelings that object gives us. When one is addicted to drugs, it's the feeling drugs give them that they are addicted too. When we are addicted to a person, it's the feelings we feel connected to them one is addicted too. When one is addicted to money it's the feelings one has that money makes them feel that they are addicted too.

The pain experienced from addiction is our inner Hell, Hell is not a physical place, and it is a state of mental torment. This torment is self-imposed and many are blind to that and blame their imprisonment on situations, events and other people.

By shining the light with understanding then one no longer has to be blind to the three worlds. Shining the light is to understand what our five basic needs are and that the reptilian brain survives through pleasure from it, and giving it those needs to prevent us from craving pleasure.

It is through the use of rational thinking to fulfill those five basic needs. Rational thinking leads to self-gratification, toward the achievement of all the good things and personal pleasures that are possible in one's life time. Ways to fulfill those needs are getting plenty of fluids; eat right, exercise and proper breathing to get the right amount of oxygen. Other ways of pleasure for example are intellectual adventures, social frolicking, voluntary love relationships, political intrigue, cultural and artistic indulgences and philosophical musings. While irrational individuals compulsively chase after short range hedonism, as I said the rational individual concentrates their energy on long term beneficial pleasure.

During the years of dependence on false gods there is very little emotional growth that is possible, because personal growth takes place when we face our fears, discomforts and anxieties. Using false gods to cope with uncomfortable emotions, including boredom prevents you from learning independent ways of thinking. You are emotionally dead while you are artificially feeling good.

Addicts are often cynical and that cynicism is really apathy and resignation to the dependence of false gods when other game plans have failed to produce emotional reward. Apathy is the unbalance energy of loving kindness.

The animal instincts which I will cover in more detail are also in the realm of blindness. As humans we are animals just like other animals except we have the function to be self-aware. We are sexual beings with a tribal instinct. The tribal instinct allows us to have each other's back. It is necessary for our survival with the limited physical attributes that we have, especially in harsh dangerous climate. Our peripheral vision is limited, we cannot see equally behind us and the front like rabbits. We cannot hear and smell like dogs and cats. Our physical bodies are not as strong or fast as many of the other animals. It is our ability to reason and our tribal instincts that keeps us alive. Our tribal instinct functions on the need to want to fit in. it allows us to have the capacity to love and wanting love. Through self-acceptance then we have no need to seek love outside our self.

This seeking the need for love is essentially someone else's opinion of you, we tend to respond to loving opinions of others with a corresponding self-opinion of our self. Looking within and accepting yourself, then there is no need to seek the need for others approval. When we look outside our self for approval, for this, need, it can lead one to become desperate for attention. When one doesn't feel they are getting their needs met, it causes pain and there is one of the two ways to handle the pain of not being validated. One is to desperately do something to get attention or do what one can to escape the emotional pain.

To be afraid of the symbolism the dark gods represent being afraid of facing oneself. Black and white thinking of believing in absolute bad and good reinforces addictions, the need to escape from our self. Walk the shadows and shine the light of Ksitigarbha to illuminate that which is hidden within you. Therefore in order to be free, one must have unconditional love of themselves which is by self-accepting of our strengths as well as our weaknesses, that is when we are truly free.

Chapter 9

Mindfulness of Hunger

There is mindful eating, such as do not watch TV or red while eating and fully experience the sensation of lifting food into your mouth, putting it in and chewing, tasting and swallowing food, and experience the pleasure.

What else one can try is mindful hunger. All the time that we think we are hungry we are not, its just craving. One must find out what is triggering the fake hunger, that may cause us to run to the fridge. It could be something we saw, or one of the other basic needs are not being fulfilled, such as not drinking enough fluids for example, or lack of oxygen due to lack of exercise.

When you pay attention to the craving, it's manageable. When it real hunger one can pay attention to the sensations in the body.

Being mindful of hunger, then one doesn't have to be reactive and immediately eat or take in whatever it is one is craving.

Hydrating oneself with water can curve many cravings. It also alleviates anxiety. Craving and anxiety share many similar attributes including comparable responses to pharmacological agents. The high correlation between craving and anxiety suggests common mechanisms underlying both. Withdrawal can cause anxiety, and anxiety can cause craving. Anxiety is fear of a change of a future outcome. When it comes to change, it brings fear of the unknown. This brings stress which causes the hormone called cortisol to go up which lowers the hormone serotonin which is the feel good hormone. Serotonin is thought to be a contributor to feelings of well-being and happiness.

When this hormone is low, we tend to crave things that will cause that hormone to rise. Regular exercise helps as well. It increases the level of tryptophan in the brain (an amino acid used to manufacture serotonin). When we don't exercise our body craves it, even if the individual despises it. Not only does exercise increase serotonin, it also releases the hormone dopamine. When we are not aware of what the body is craving, we can mistake it as hunger for something else. Being dehydrated can cause an increase in anxiety and cravings. Our body is thirsty, though if you are not aware exactly what your body wants, it can lead to trying to get that longing fulfilled with something else.

Such things as dehydration, lack of exercise, lack of meditation can manifest as cravings because our body depends on those hormones that those activities release to give us a sense of well-being.

One of the hormones that meditation releases is DMT, or N,N-Dimethyltryptamine. It is a naturally occurring chemical found in both plants and animals. It is the active hallucinogenic compound in such teas such as ayahuasca.

Meditation produces such a low amount, not enough to hallucinate, though enough to give a sense of well-being and insight about our self. Meditation allows one to be more aware in watching one's thoughts. Even though I'm not condoning the use of ayahuasca, this tea has produced hallucinations that give one more insight about themselves. A user may suddenly look at themselves different than they ever did before. One may hallucinate friendly snakes gently wrapping around them, and then come to the realization that the snakes are themselves and see themselves suddenly as a mother would, and gain insight that they need to have more compassion towards themselves and not commit violent acts against oneself by settling with people who don't have their best interest.

Being aware that they are hallucinations may cause one to integrate unity within themselves, just like when one realizes the deities in the after death are hallucinations they integrate unity. Believing they are external separate from one self is no different than having a bad acid trip.

When those hormones are low, it can cause us to feel empty. That emptiness feeling can cause a longing that doesn't end. As long as we seek externally to fill that longing, and don't get to the source of the cause, it will always lead to a feeling of longing with no satisfaction.

Chapter 10
The Split

The monsters we create symbolize the fears we have about our self. We were all born whole. That wholeness is short-lived because we are relationally dependent as children. Being born relationally dependent into families that indoctrinate into us of what aspects of ourselves are acceptable and others are not. What is acceptable versus unacceptable depends upon the perspective of the family and society we are born into.

The aspects of ourselves that are seen as unacceptable, both positive and negative, are rejected by our families, and the aspects that are seen as acceptable are not. So, being relationally dependent in the name of survival, we do anything we can to disown, deny, or suppress those aspects in ourselves that are disapproved of. This creates a split within a person which is called the conscious and the subconscious. This self-preservation instinct of dividing ourselves into conscious and subconscious is in fact our first act of self-rejection.

In the 20th century psychologist Carl Jung was studying with Freud, and they together noticed that people had a conscious aspect and a subconscious aspect. This means an individual can has aspects of themselves they are aware of, and aspects they are entirely unaware of.

Consciousness has long been referred to as a light. To become aware of something, you have to be able to see it in the same way that you might see something that is suddenly illuminated in light. When something is unconscious, you can't see it, because you are unaware of it. The same way that you are unaware of something that might be in a dark room because the darkness is there, you can't see it. So, what Jung began to do is refer to the aspects of a person that they themselves are unaware of, or unconscious of as the shadow. So, the human shadow is any aspect of a person that is not exposed to the light of their own consciousness.

Freud speculated that there are parts of the unconscious one can never know about, this is not so, the parts we don't know, are caused by the split, the split that can be unite by purging the indoctrination we have been influence by since childhood.

The reason that the hidden shadow aspects of us contains mostly what we would consider negative things is because most of us tend to deny, suppress, disown, or reject aspects of ourselves that we feel are negative. The truth is that all those things we think are negative are not. Many of the aspects that are rejected are truly positive. This is definitely true with those who struggle with shame and low self-opinion of themselves.

Here is an example of how something that is not negative ends up in the hidden shadow within the subconscious. A girl is born with a sense of self, she knows who she is, she knows what she likes, she is attracted to other girls, she knows exactly what she doesn't like and she for sure speaks her opinion. Her family she came from think little girls should not be seen and not heard, and only be with boys of her own race. She feels to get the love and acceptance from her family, to be this sweet little girl who doesn't speak her mind. The aspects of herself that is assertive and confident are not accepted by her family, not only that, she is told its wrong to attracted to other women, especially those outside her race. Therefore for the sake of survival so she can fit in, she will begin to learn to reject those aspects of herself. In order to get love as an adult. She winds up being this sweet obedient girl who dates only men of her race. Her life will be painful because she has exiled that part of herself, she is divided.

She may eventually come to the realization what she was indoctrinated with was not right and discover her what feelings, beliefs, or memories are part of her subconscious and discover that she is in fact, assertive and confident and attracted to women of a different ethnicity than her own. When she reclaims that part of herself, she can be confident, assertive and happy as she accepts who she really is, through self-acceptance and date whomever she wants.

Here is an example of how the negative aspects end up in the hidden in the shadow. A child feels anger and they are born in a family that says anger is wrong and a sin. So now when that child feels anger, they are shamed for feeling that emotion and punished for it.

Now that child grows up and tries to dissociate themselves from that anger in every way that they can, but the anger doesn't go away, one just consciously denied it, and it becomes repressed and in the subconscious. As an adult this person will most likely not have any awareness that he has any anger in him at all. He will not and cannot see himself clearly because he has denied that aspect of himself. So, when people tell him, "Man, you're really angry, I can feel the anger in you," he will not relate to that at all. He will probably relate to himself as easygoing. Meanwhile his anger may be turned inward as depression. Inside he is very angry, because he was shamed for having anger, he holds things in and doesn't express himself. Therefore he doesn't get his needs met due to poor communication which feeds his anger. That anger is turned inward wearing the mask of depression.

If he works with someone to discover the feelings, beliefs, and memories that are part of his subconscious, he may discover that he truly is angry, and that anger has been coming all along in passive-aggressive ways that are hurting himself and those around him. He also finds out that his depression is also anger. If he addresses the anger directly, his passive-aggressive behavior will cease to exist and his human relationships will become more enjoyable.

When we deny, disown or suppress something it doesn't disappear, it just fades from our conscious awareness into the world of blindness which is the subconscious. This is the real reason why most people do so many things in life that they don't understand what they are doing. It's why most people are still completely out of control of themselves.

The reason why people reject facing those hidden parts is because to acknowledge something that you have suppressed in your subconscious mind, because you have rejected and denied it, you must come face to face with the pain of having to fracture yourself and lose an aspect of yourself for the sake of being loved.

What caused the pain of rejection originally will come up every time you do inner work to bring light to the dark. In other words, it will bring up the same feeling of rejection that we were met with the first time around from our parents and caregivers, and so it makes us feel like we are going to be exiled or punished again. It sets off survival mechanisms, and thus makes us feel like we are literally going to die. It's no wonder self-awareness is not so easy to attain. Many who are still caught up in duality concept of "I" versus others will use the excuse it's too dark and that they rather stay in the light. This dualism causes one to lean toward literalism and the beliefs in absolute evil and good. With this attitude what's in the dark, will remain in the world of blindness, as it subconsciously continue to control us.

Every human in existence that was ever socialized, which is pretty much everyone on earth, has gone through this process of splitting themselves into parts, splitting themselves into conscious and subconscious. This self-rejection is the birth of self-hatred, and the emptiness that we feel is the remainder that's left over of those aspects of ourselves that we have suppressed.

Humans will be presented with every single opportunity to see the aspects of themselves they have denied. We will be provided with every single opportunity to confront our demons. So, it matters not how far we run, or try to hide, our shadow will keep chasing us until we are willing to do the work that must be done with it. This is to do the work of bringing light to that which was hidden in the shadow.

Unfortunately, facing the dark has become a rather controversial process, because it is painful. It is true that self-awareness does not come naturally to those who make a practice of avoiding pain, because to become aware of those aspects, you must stop trying to escape the pain and emptiness within you where those missing parts should be. Trying to avoid this reality is what causes that eternal hunger, the hunger that the hungry ghost realm symbolizes. Facing the dark is the key to a consciously aware and free life.

The more aware you are of your worlds of blindness, the more embodied you are as a conscious being. No one has ever reached enlightenment without confronting their hidden shadow and exposing it to the light of consciousness.

Entering the underworld, the subconscious is the work of bringing attention and love to those aspects of yourself that have been previously denied.

We all want to be loved. Seeking love outside our self leads to suffering. The shame from family indoctrination is a wedge between love and self. Remember, not self-cherishing which is an image mask to hide self-loathing. Like the examples of the children I mentioned, conformed to their parents' indoctrination to get their acceptance. Both children in the examples grew up feeling pain of not being who they really are. Living her life conforming, she felt a longing, emptiness inside. The man with the anger issues also experiences this longing. Sometimes to deal with the pain of not getting our needs met, we get a craving for something and use that to try to feel the void.

We all want to be loved. Seeking love outside our self leads to suffering. Like the woman I mentioned in previous paragraph, conformed to her parents' indoctrination to get their acceptance. She grew up feeling pain of not being who she really is. Living her life conforming, she felt a longing, emptiness inside. Sometimes to deal with the pain of not getting our needs met, we get a craving for something and use that to try to feel the void.

There within us is an instinct to want to love and be loved. When we do love our self, it causes us to achieve the things we deserve to have. As we have self-respect and show respect to each other by enjoying the fruits of our labor, we show compassion to others. In response we receive the recognition that we desired. Therefore we have the ability to love and be loved.

On the other hand, those who lack the ability to love themselves, have a void inside. They seek outside themselves to fill a void that can never be filled. To receive recognition becomes a desperate journey. It becomes a dangerous journey when one is reactive and willing to do anything to get noticed. When the ego is weak, its yells out, "Look at me, look at me, notice me, I'm right here," when one is desperate to get noticed, you have people who do stupid things to get that 15 minutes of fame when they gun down a crowd. Irrational impulsive people will steal, cheat, lie, murder and commit all kinds of heinous acts in order to be noticed.

As humans we don't want to be ignored. Humans would even settle with bad attention than to receive no attention at all. If a parent ignores their child, not given them the love they crave, that child will act out and get attention, even if it's bad attention. Being yelled at and scolded is better than nothing to the one seeking attention. When individuals feel like they are not getting the attention, many turn to other things to escape from the pain. They seek what they can to fit in, or just escape all together filling in the void.

It is this instinct within us that influences cultures and where people are located. This instinct wants us to fit in. Different demographic areas of the USA for example, are more dominated more with ideas than others. In New Orleans there are a high percentage of homosexuals. In the South on the Bible belt, is more religious than other areas of the USA. In other areas it's more New Age populace. It is this tribal instinct within us to want to fit in is responsible. We are either influenced by our peers or we move and gravitate closer to like-minded. Our tribal instinct can work for us and also work against us. Example, if an individual are hanging around plenty of alcoholics, due to the tribal instinct to want to fit in, that individual may start out just drinking occasionally socially. Before they know it they find themselves gradually drinking more and more, before they know it, they have a drinking problem.

On the other hand it works the other way. In anonymous meetings such as Alcoholics Anonymous the power at the core to staying sober is the bond with similar people, this bond due to that tribal instinct causes us to want to fit in. when one bonds with other sober individuals, the thought of using is not even conceived. Those people in the bonding circle become the individual's world. The thought of using is not conceived, because it's like being the only one in the world using. That thought in itself is lonely. By my experience, when I had just a few people I was close to that was clean and sober, I didn't want to use. I didn't want to be the only one in the world using. Those who I'm not close to I knew doesn't exist in my world. Loneliness can be dangerous, because when you feel, lonely, then you are the only one in the world that exists from the individual's perspective. In this state of mind, it's easy to use because it doesn't matter to the individual if they feel no one else exist in their world anyway. Therefore it is the bonding is the strength in meetings. Some people don't connect, don't bond, and that is why AA works for some and not for others.

It is also this instincts which is the ego that causes us to use and also causes us to say, "enough is enough." This is another way how it works for us or against us. We want to be able to love and be loved. When we feel we are not getting our needs met, it's easy to become frustrated and use something to escape that pain. People then become addicts as a way to fill that void they long for, a void that cannot be filled, until one learns to love themselves.

The same applies to serial killers. There are three types of serial killers. One type kills for thrill, it satisfies his/hers addiction for a short time, killing to fill that void with a short high. These ones take longer to get caught for they try their best to dispose of the victim's body so it won't be found. Their killing is their choice of drug from the thrill. The attention seeker serial killer will leave the body displayed so that it can be found. He wants people to know what he done, even if he hides his identity. He seeks attention from others, which is his high, so he must display the bodies. He seeks attention, even if it's bad attention. This type would prefer to be hated by most then not to be noticed at all, even though he would prefer to be loved by all. The third type is just careless and sloppy because he is too disorganized due to mental disorders.

The same applies to terrorist and all warmongers. Terrorist want everyone to know what they did to create terror. This is the attention they seek. Warmongers want attention by wanting everyone to see that they are right and everyone is wrong. Invading countries is their way if proving they are right. This is the term Might Is Right, or The Survival of the Fittest by author Ragnar Redbeard. This is the concept that only strength or physical might can establish moral rights. Throughout history when a country is invaded, those who win consider their gods the true gods and they establish moral rights. The cultures that lost the war, their gods are then demonized.

To know and understand ourselves we must go deep into the subconscious mind. Going inward is what is needed to achieve mastery which brings joy in one's life.

When we are grounded in reality, seeing reality as it is, we come to realizing that it's not about seeking peace, because there are always challenges, instead to seek victory by always challenging ourselves that is by being better than we were yesterday. Being grounded is being in the moment; realizing that the past, present and future are the same. If we always see our desired goal in the future it will always be in the future where we never reach. Instead we have to see what we want, as if it has already been granted. When we treat things as if our desires have already been granted, our behavior choices are different. We make different decisions when we have already achieved something than when we think it's in the far future. When we see it's already been granted, then we take actions to preserve and keep what we are grateful for. When we do this, we can enjoy the pleasures of achieving wealth prosperity and happiness.

Chapter 11
The Taming of Yama

In the myth, Yama, the Lord of Death drank the blood from the cups made from the skulls of the thieves he killed, and then decided to kill everyone in Tibet, because he was angry and upset that the thieves interrupted his 50 years of meditation.

The people of Tibet were afraid for their lives and prayed to Manjushri. Manjushri transformed into Yamantaka and defeated Yama and tamed him to be the protector of Buddhism.

Yama means death and Yamantaka means "Destroyer of Death." In Buddhism the goal is to annihilate the ego. This doesn't mean to completely rid of the ego as many believe. It is to get rid of self-cherishing. Annihilating the ego is more like taming the ego, like Yamantaka destroys Yama, by taming him.

When one is caught up in the "I" versus others, the ego is in survival mode. In survival mode, one then manifest anger and greed, this breeds all the other unhealthy emotions which cause us to be dead inside. We must have a clear understanding of life itself in order to live life to the fullest.

The real secret is to 'die' while still alive, consciously allowing ourselves to transcend 'I'-ness in order to become universal. Meditation can also be called the process of conscious annihilation. The ego is then tamed and no longer manifesting self-cherishing as one then begins to understand interdependence. One begins to the idea of transcending the 'I'-ness with love. When this happens, we succeed in annihilating or taming the ego, which was creating restriction and not letting life blossom.

With this transcendence of ego, we experience liveliness for the first time. What is liveliness? It means to live life with a heart; a life that is now connected to the eternal and the immortal; a life where there is neither bliss nor sorrow. With such a transformation comes the wisdom to conduct life with self- discipline.

This transcendence of the ego is symbolized by Yama being tamed. In this state the ego has no need to puff itself up. One has no need to be right over others.

Yama who is sometimes called the King of Hell is a dharmapala (wrathful god). In the Theravādin tradition of Buddhism, he is portrayed as sending old age, disease, punishments, and other calamities among humans as warnings to behave well.

As a dharmapala which means Defenders of the Law (Dharma), or the Protectors of the Law, he resides in the realm of the narakas (hells).

When we allow ourselves to jump into the depths of consciousness, many people become frightened. They fail to understand the real goal of what is taking place.
When we are born we descend into our body and become trapped in our head. This is the underworld, the tomb which is our body.

The dead are those who walk around daily ruled by the illusions of limitations which are self-imposed. The dead are those who are trapped in trying to fit in with everyone where they cease to no longer be an individual. They are part of the system. The light within, which is the true you has been ruled all of your life by Hell. Now it is time to rise from the pit of self-imposed limitations.

When you go into meditation and enter into the subconscious, you are Yamantaka imitating Yama (Death) in order to conquer death and ascend back to the living to be alive.

Conquering death is also about overcoming the fear of death. Death is tamed when one doesn't fear death.

As I mentioned cravings are caused by imbalances in the body chemistry cause by numerous things such as poor diet, stress, lack of exercise and lack of meditation. When we look outside our self, that craving is also validation, craving to be validated.

Example, you may be in a relationship and a attractive single person asks you for a cup of coffee. You are excited about it. Now the question is, is it really about the cup of coffee? What are you looking for? What's going on in your relationship that you are out with someone else for a cup of coffee?

It's not the coffee one is seeking, it is validation. It is the ego needing to be validated by someone else to make one feel good. To do this, the craving is attention, unless you are addicted to caffeine. Craving this attention is letting in an opening where the most seemingly harmless decisions are wrought with life changing consequences.

Being approached by the attractive person in this scenario is your Dharma giving you an opportunity to grow a step towards Buddhahood. To not see this opportunity or test and go have the cup of coffee with this person, just made your power to resist temptation even harder for the next thing that comes next.

On the flip side you may mistake something as a test when it is not. Example is that you are away from your spouse on business, and an attractive associate ask you to join him in his room later. You decline and walk away, proud of yourself that you resisted. Was there any challenge? You have a wonderful spouse at home, great children and a comfortable life. You may have been flattered, though turning it down, didn't cost you much. That may not been the test, perhaps it's possible that the challenge was to overcome your self-cherishing. It would be like the scenario when the first individual named Tenzin wasn't tempted by the money he saw in the room and then took pride that he didn't take it. This pride is unproductive for it serves no purpose, it is self-cherishing, it is the 'I'-ness saying, "look at me, look what I done, I'm important" this is just craving for self-exalting which is just narcissism or self-righteousness.

On the other hand, if the same scenario took every ounce to say "no" from your lips as you fantasized about what you would be missing, then you are taking a step overcoming your self-cherishing.

Death was personified in early yoga, as the Kaṭha Upaniṣad. There are many complex myths about Yama's origin, role, and activities, but one in particular was deeply important in early Yoga history, narrated in the beautiful

Kaṭha Upaniṣad, from around 1000-500 BCE. The Kaṭha tells the story of a young seeker named Naciketas who, after an argument with his father about the proper conduct of a sacrifice, is cursed by him, and walks to the home of Death (Yama) to inquire after the truth. Upon arriving, he finds nobody home, and waits for 3 days. When Yama returns, he praises the boy for his bravery, apologizes for not treating him as a guest should be treated, and offers 3 boons (wishes to be fulfilled).

For the first boon, Naciketas asks to be returned home alive and restored to his father's graces. This is about the necessity to resolve conflict in our intimate relationships before deeper spiritual work can proceed.

For the second boon, Naciketas asks for the secret to the fire sacrifice (yajña). Yama teaches him the form and chants in exhaustive detail, and upon hearing the instructions repeated back perfectly, declares Naciketas a master of the form, so much so that the sacrifice itself will now be named after the boy: the Naciketas Sacrifice. This layer is about discipline, learning, purification, and precision.

The third boon, Naciketas seems to get in trouble. He asks for the secret to what lies after death, whether people exist after they die. Death resists answering and offers Naciketas wealth, power, sensual pleasures, and long life as replacement prizes. Naciketas refuses, saying that all those things are also under Yama's power (i.e.: will inevitably die), and he wants the way beyond Yama's power. This resonates with other myths of a spiritual seeker being met at the eve of liberation by a figure who tries to pull them off their path through offering material comforts, Jesus in the desert and the Buddha under the Bodhi Tree are examples. Yama finally relents, offering the first systematic contemplative practice to be called "yoga", Adhyātma Yoga, "Yoga of the Deep Self", and a long, beautiful wisdom teaching on the true identity of the Soul/Self, or Ātman.

In the Kaṭha, Yama appears as the Guru, the ultimate teacher. But how can the same figure be both the teacher and the thing the seeker wants to be free from? Death seems to resist Naciketas' demand for the secret of birth-and-death, but then he admits that he was just testing him, saying that most seekers succumb at that point and accept worldly power instead of the path to wisdom. Yama praises Naciketas' steadfastness, and in his instructions on yoga invokes the all-important practice that Naciketas has already demonstrated: not to be swayed by pleasures or reactive to pain. Naciketas already has the great yogic quality of composure, and now just needs a View teaching, which he gets, to realize the truth.

In Buddhism Māra (literally "death") appears in the Pali texts as a semi-divine figure who confronts the Buddha both before and after his liberation, and many monks and nuns periodically, always with the intent to cause them to doubt their actions or in some way interrupt their practice. Stories of practitioners meeting, and invariably recognizing and thus dispelling, Māra fill a chapter in the Samyutta

Nikaya, as well as appearing regularly in other sutta (sutra) collections. Māra continues to figure in the Mahāyāna literature as well, and his role develops substantially.

Māra's known appearance is in the *Buddhacarita*, "Life of the Buddha" (BC), and the Lalitavistara (LV), of the Sarvastivada School.

In these, Gotama (the not-yet-Buddha) is visited by Māra as he sits under the Bodhi Tree on the eve of liberation. Māra has already visited the Buddha at key points in his search, including an attempt to dissuade him from leaving home to begin it. Now Māra tries to dissuade the Buddha from proceeding to liberation, shooting at him with the arrow of sensual desire (the same flower-tipped arrow that caused Śambhu (Śiva) to lose his yogic discipline and succumb to lust), and sending his sexy daughters, named Lust, Delight, and Thirst (*Rati, Priti,* and *Tṛṣna* in the BC; *Rati, Arati,* and *Tṛṣna* in the LV) to seduce him. Māra sends in a vicious army of demons, who also fail to budge the sage.

In the LV, a source for the most iconic moment in the myth, Māra tries doubt, his signature weapon throughout the Pāli texts: he tries to convince Gotama that he has no right to become free — meaning "free from me",

Since Gotama has said from the beginning that he seeks "the deathless". In the iconic moment of victory, the Buddha wordlessly reaches down and touches the Earth, symbolically calling on the Divine Feminine to bear witness to his aeons of practice and cultivation of the Perfections (*parami*), and thus his "right" to awaken. The goddess appears, offers her earthquake-triggering witness, and Māra is vanquished.

The earth as the witness is vindication of our own right to be here, and to practice for freedom. The earth as our witness called the *Bhumisparśa Mudra* ("Earth-witness Mudra") is an assertion of self-worth. As long as we are alive, we are worthy. The cravings to fill in a void are symbolic of the blind world of hunger besides hormonal imbalances are craving to be loved. Wanting to fit in, seeking attention are ways that we settle less for because we are looking for love externally. As long as we continue to seek externally for this that void, that empty feeling will always be there. This will cause attachments in the form of addictions (greed) and manifest in all kinds of behaviors that will hurt yourself and others.

Māra and Yama both symbolizes Death. The difference between Yama isn't evil at all in the Veda, but an important governing deity, and clearly in the Kaṭha isn't trying to deceive Naciketas as Māra is the Buddha.

But there are some interesting parallels between the two myths:

1. Both Naciketas and Gotama set out on their quests motivated by an initial encounter with death: Naciketas through his father's curse, and Gotama through the 4 Heavenly Messengers (old age, sickness, death, and the wandering ascetic).

2. Both upset their parents when they leave.

3. Both meet the personification of death once they've proven their fortitude and sat in a place of retreat fasting for some time. Naciketas sits in Yama's house for 3 days without food or water. Gotama sits under the bodhi tree after years of ascetic fasting (and *almost* dying, thus we could say poetically "visiting the house of Death").

In Gotama's case, his fast is ended by his admission that it has failed to succeed at liberating him, and his insight that pleasurable meditation (*jhāna*) will be a more successful method. He then takes some food from Sujata, a local woman offering alms, and sits under the tree after his strength is restored. In Naciketas's case, Yama tells him that being left without food is no way to treat an honored guest, and apologizes. In both cases, fasting is criticized, once on social grounds for Naciketas, and once on efficacy grounds for Gotama.

4. Both master an existing religious salvation system, are praised for doing so, then decide it's not sufficient and aim higher. Naciketas masters the Vedic sacrificial ritual (*yajña*), then asks for the wisdom that understands what happens after death, which turns out to be attained through the practice of *samādhi* based in sense-withdrawal (the meditative skill formalized called *pratyāhāra*). Gotama masters formless meditative concentration under two local teachers (*samādhi*, also based in sense-withdrawal, since the two states he learns are characterized by "nothingness" and "neither-perception-nor-non-perception"), but sees

that it's not sufficient in itself and goes in search of a full end of suffering, which will entail specific inquiry/contemplations (*vipassanā*).

5. Before the true breakthrough to inquiry and liberation, both are tempted by Death through the offer of sensual objects. Naciketas is offered wealth, power, long life, beautiful women with chariots and musical instruments, and the fulfillment of all worldly desires. Gotama is offered essentially the same, starting with the promise that Gotama would conquer "the lower worlds" with arrows and "gain the higher worlds of Indra", implying the power and wealth of earthly kingship followed by the long-lived pleasures of heaven. When that fails, Māra sends in his seducing daughters. (The Buddhist texts then add a battle, with Māra sending in an army.

6. In the Buddhist story, Māra is dispelled, leaving Gotama alone to pursue his inquiry. In the Katha, Yama gives in and begins teaching. This may signify the same thing. For Naciketas, Yama as Tempter and Enemy is vanquished, and only Yama as Teacher remains. For Gotama, Māra as Tempter and Enemy is vanquished, and his independent power of samadhi and inquiry remains. After his realization, the Buddha will proclaim that he has no teacher, and this contributes to his social status as outside any of the existing spiritual lineages.

Contemplation on Death

Reflecting on the inevitability of our own death and meditation on images of dead bodies in states of decay are central Buddhist practices. The first is a practice known as The Five Reflections, drawn from this sutta. Here's an English version to chant every day:

I am of the nature to age, I have not gone beyond ageing.
I am of the nature to sicken, I have not gone beyond
sickness.
I am of the nature to die, I have not gone beyond dying.
All that is mine, beloved and pleasing, will become
otherwise, will become separated from me.
I am the owner of my kamma, heir to my kamma, born of
my kamma, related to my kamma, abide supported by my
kamma. Whatever kamma I shall do, for good or for ill, of
that I will be the heir.
(from the Abhayagiri monastic chant book)

The corpse contemplations are part of a practice called Mindfulness of Death, which in Pali is *Māranasati*, or "Remembering Māra". "Remembering", the practitioner "remembers", meaning is intimately aware of, their body and that of others in terms of the breath, movements and postures, parts of the body, the experience of the 4 great elements, and the images of a corpse in decay. The whole series teaches in a systematic way that this body is headed in one direction only! In addition to the body contemplations, the practitioner trains in awareness of the core feelings of pleasant and unpleasant (again, to become conscious of how habitually we react to them), then the awareness of wholesome and unwholesome states of mind, then a series of important qualities of mind and heart to cultivate on the path, culminating with awareness of teaching of the 4 Noble Truths.

Death is the teacher because death is what guides the search, and the insight into death's power is the insight that the Canon describes practitioners exclaiming when they awaken suddenly: All that is subject to arising is subject to passing away. The insight into impermanence is a humble bow to death, and the end of denial, resistance, and fear.

Gotama's third insight was the insight into suffering (*dukkha*) and its end through the uprooting of its causes which is clinging to things that are impermanence. All things die, no matter what, nothing stays the same, therefore it's unhealthy to cling to anything even though we can fully enjoy everything in the moment.

In a story a woman named Kisa Gotami was grieving insanely for the death of her child. She went around asking for medicine for her child, people kept telling her that her child is dead. She was in denial and said, " No no no, he is just sick." Eventually a kind man said to her," Go to the Buddha, for he is the great healer." The woman went to the Buddha. He told her he would heal her if she can get white mustard seeds from a house where no one has ever died. She went on a journey to get this mustard seed. She desperately went from house to house, and disappointed to find out that in each house someone had died and Kisa Gotami actions reminded each household of their grief. Finally the realization struck her that there is no house free from mortality. She then eventually let go and sought refuge.

Even though we may be suffering, it's an opportunity to see clear through whole structure of condition existence. Pain, suffering makes one look deeply into the depths of existence itself. Dukkha is the first of the four noble truths, the first stage of the spiritual path. It causes us to search to get to the root and cause of the problem, remember "Hell is the lama for all Buddhas".

The realm of the hungry ghost as I discussed is symbolic of what goes on inside when we are constantly craving. In the story, the ghost with their large saucer shaped eyes and big stomachs cannot get any food down. They are on a endless search for food and water. When they try to drink water it turns into fire, and when they come across deliciously good looking food, it turns into excrement in their mouths and as they try to swallow it, it turns into razor blades and thorns as it lacerates their throats. A gnawing hunger is always there and they see with their huge yes, that satisfaction is always over there. The hungry ghosts are always scurrying always searching endlessly with no rest for food.

The answer to ending that suffering of the realm of hungry ghost is Amitabha. Amitabha is a celestial Buddha according to the scriptures of Mahāyāna Buddhism. Amitābha is the principal Buddha in Pure Land Buddhism. In Vajrayana Buddhism, Amitābha is known for his longevity attribute, magnetizing red fire element, the conglomerate of discernment, pure perception and the deep awareness of emptiness of all.

Amitābha means "Infinite Light" so Amitābha is also called "The Buddha of Immeasurable Life and Light". So while the brilliant red light of Discriminating Wisdom shines from Amitābha, the dull yellow comforting light of craving shines from the realm of the hungry ghosts. The dull yellow light is of the element earth. This is the everyday average conscious state, most of us find this comfortable because it's not foreign to us. It's our comfort zone. Due to this comfort zone, many are afraid to change, for the fear of losing their false identity and facing the unknown.

In this state is the mind state of consistent cravings. The huge eyes of the hungry ghost symbolizes us always looking for satisfaction and how our eyes deceive us by how good something looks. We fool our self into thinking what we see will satisfy our craving. Are eyes big thinking, maybe if I have money I will be happy, or if I have that big screen TV then I will be happy, or if I'm with such and such in a relationship, then I will be happy. It's never satisfied because craving is endless. We become like the hungry ghost as long as we continual to look outside our self for fulfillment.

The brilliant red light of Discriminating Wisdom from Amitābha is of the element fire. Fire symbolizes the intellectual faculty and the ability to "discern, judge, comprehend, and understand". In sanskrit it would be Buddhi. In Tibet there are five elements in Tibetan Medicine is traditionally called Sowa Rigpa, meaning "The

Science of Healing". It has its own standardized systems of anatomy, physiology, pathology, diagnosis, and treatment.

Figure 5 Amitābha of the Pure Land Buddhism

It is also intimately linked with the spiritual philosophy of Buddhism, and elemental astrology science. The five elements in Tibetan Buddhism are earth, water, fire, air, and space.

When it comes to the brilliant red light of Discriminating Wisdom, give thought your purpose, Discriminate and see what the path is and what is not the path. Bring awareness to the craving. Where is this craving leading too and if I follow this craving, will it lead me to my destination? Those cravings come in many forms, drugs, food sex, religious experiences, none of those things will fulfill that craving. In all these things we are looking for is affection, love. You can only get love if you yourself are a loving person. Perhaps deep within we want to give love, express love it with creativity. One must have to love themselves in order to give love to others. One can only give what they have. If one is filled with self-loathing, then they lack the capacity to love others. Some of their actions may mimic love, though it's actually for themselves due to fear of loss. In the end, it's not love and others get hurt.

Here is an allegory that shows what causes hell or the realm of the eternal hunger. This story is called the "The Parable of the Long Spoons."

I once ascended to the firmaments. I first went to see Hell and the sight was horrifying. Row after row of tables were laden with platters of sumptuous food, yet the people seated around the tables were pale and emaciated, moaning in hunger. As I came closer, I understood their predicament.

Every person held a full spoon, but both arms were splinted with wooden slats so he could not bend either elbow to bring the food to his mouth. It broke my heart to hear the tortured groans of these poor people as they held their food so near but could not consume it.

Next I went to visit Heaven. **I was surprised to see the same setting I had witnessed in Hell** - row after row of long tables laden with food. But in contrast to Hell, the people here in Heaven were sitting contentedly talking with each other, obviously sated from their sumptuous meal.

As I came closer, I was amazed to discover that here, too, each person had his arms splinted on wooden slats that prevented him from bending his elbows. How, then, did they manage to eat?

As I watched, a man picked up his spoon and dug it into the dish before him. Then he stretched across the table and fed the person across from him! The recipient of this kindness thanked him and returned the favor by leaning across the table to feed his benefactor.

I suddenly understood. **Heaven and Hell offer the same circumstances and conditions. The critical difference is in the way the people treat each other. Love only requires one skill. These people learned early on to share and feed one another. While the greedy only think of themselves.**

I ran back to Hell to share this solution with the poor souls trapped there. I whispered in the ear of one starving man, 'You do not have to go hungry. Use your spoon to feed your neighbor, and he will surely return the favor and feed you.'

'You expect me to feed the detestable man sitting across the table?' said the man angrily. 'I would rather starve than give him the pleasure of eating!'

Sometimes, thinking solely of our personal gratification, we tend to forget our interdependence with everyone and everything around us, so much so that we stop caring about them. But, as the parable makes it clear, by doing so, not only don't we help others overcome their suffering, but we're also unconsciously harming ourselves, since we are all connected on a very deep level.

When we are craving endlessly, we are being self-cherishing. We do not see the interdependent of others. All we see is fulfilling our next fix. The deeper the hunger, the more desperate and the less regards we have for others.

Love comes from within, we must take care and have compassion towards our self so that we can express love to others. This acknowledgment is called Ahimsa, which is the first of the five vows of the seeker. Ahimsa means nonviolence.

The first step of yama begins with love. The fundamental divine law that governs life is "Love all". If the idea of hurting someone remains in the heart, you have failed in the first step itself. Love selflessly, unconditionally and joyfully. This is the essence of ahimsa.

It is a simple matter to understand that liking someone ultimately culminates in love. When we love all, where is the question of being violent or hurting others? When we love, we are ready to sacrifice our comforts, our possessions and ultimately ourselves. It is sad that under the spell of hatred, people destroy each other. This also means not to commit violence acts against yourself. To see yourself as worthless is violent acts against yourself, harming any one is violent acts against yourself since we are all interdependent.

There are some mantras to do to help with getting in touch with our Buddha nature in order to express the embodiment of compassion. This is explained in the next chapter.

Chapter 12
Mantra

Tibetan Buddhists believe that saying the mantra (chant), Om Mani Padme Hum, out loud or silently to oneself, invokes the embodiment of compassion. Spinning the written form of the mantra around in a Mani wheel (or prayer wheel) is also believed to give the same benefit as saying the mantra, and Mani wheels, small hand wheels and large wheels with millions of copies of the mantra inside, are found everywhere in the lands influenced by Tibetan Buddhism.

It is said that all the teachings of the Buddha are contained in this mantra: Om Mani Padme Hum and cannot really be translated into a simple phrase or sentence. The simplest translation is "Hail to the jewel in the lotus." This is phrase has so much deeper meaning. This mantra is the most widely used of all Buddhist mantras, and open to anyone who feels inspired to practice it.

This is how it is written and pronounced.

Om	*Ma*	*Ni*	*Pad*	*Me*	*Hum*
(ohm)	(mah)	(nee)	(pahd)	(may)	(hum)

The vowel in the sylable Hu (is pronounced as in the English word 'book'. The final consonant in that syllable is often pronounced 'ng' as in 'song' -- Om Mani Padme Hung. There is one further complication: The syllablePad is pronounced Pe (peh) by many Tibetans: Om Mani Peme Hung.

All of the Dharma is based on Buddha's discovery that suffering is unnecessary: Like a illness, once we really face the fact that suffering exists, we can look more deeply and discover its cause; and when we discover that the cause is dependent on certain conditions, we can explore the possibility of removing those conditions.

When saying the mantra we connect with the body and voice and mind of the Buddha by the three aspects of the practice. Our posture and certain gestures we connect with the body, by reciting the words of the liturgy and by repeating the mantra we connect with the voice and feel the embodiment of compassion within you, feel and know that you have the Buddha potential to solve your own problems and those of others. Knowing this, you feel your infinite potential to rewrite the script in your life and solve any problem.

The entire Dharma, the entire truth about the nature of suffering and the many ways of removing its causes, is said to be contained in these six syllables in the manta.

The first word, OM, is composed of three pure letters, A, U, and M. These symbolize the practitioner's impure body, speech, and mind; and symbolize the pure exalted body, speech and mind of a Buddha. This means that our impure state can be transformed into a pure state.

MANI is the next four syllables. It means Jewel which symbolizes the intention to become enlightened, compassion and love without being self-centered on our self. It is about sharing like the parable of long sppons in the scenario where they fed each other. Like a actual jewel can remove poverty, so can the mind who thinks of others remove the poverty, which is the endless cravings. It can end this mental poverty where we can become enlightened beings.

The syllables, PADME, meaning lotus, symbolize wisdom. Just as a lotus grows forth from mud but is not sullied by the faults of mud. There is wisdom in understanding that all is impermanence and realize the emptiness of duality. Therefore even going thru challenges, we can be like a lotus and not have our mind soiled by it. The **lotus** flower is the fundamental **law** that permeates life and the universe. It is the eternal truth.

Purity must be achieved by an indivisible unity of method and wisdom, symbolized by the final syllable, HUM, which indicates indivisibility. According to the sutra system, this indivisibility of method and wisdom refers to as the Eternal Supreme and Ultimate Reality. It is the One Immutable Essence and Energy which is Existence Itself and which is itself entirely unmoved and unaffected by anything, regardless of whether the Universe is in existence at the time or not.

In terms of the seed syllables of the five conqueror Buddhas, HUM is the seed syllable of Akshobhya- the immovable, the unfluctuating consciousness that permeates existence, that which cannot be disturbed by anything.

"Thus the six syllables, OM MANI PADME HUM, mean that in dependence on the practice which is in indivisible union of method and wisdom, you can transform your impure body, speech and mind into the pure body, speech, and mind of a Buddha. It is said that you should not seek for Buddhahood outside of yourself; the substances for the achievement of Buddhahood are within." - Dalai Lama

Within the Japanese tradition such as Nicherin and Tendai Buddhism there is a mantra they chant that pretty much has the same meaning as the Tibetan "Om Mani Padme Hum". In these Japanese traditions, the mantra is Nam-myoho-renge-kyo *Devotion to the Mystic Law of the Lotus Sutra* or *Glory to the Sutra of the Lotus of the Supreme Law.*

It is to realize that Buddhas are able to solve their own problems and those of others. The Mystic Law which is the lotus transforms the life of anyone that means everyone, no matter how unhappy one is, and transforms their life into supreme happiness.

Part Three
Animal

Chapter 13
The Human Animal

The position and treatment of animals in Buddhism is important for the light it sheds on Buddhists' perception of their own relation to the natural world, on Buddhist humanitarian concerns in general, and on the relationship between Buddhist concepts and Buddhist practice.

Animals have always been regarded in Buddhist thought as sentient beings. Furthermore, animals possess Buddha nature (according to the Mahāyāna school) and therefore potential for enlightenment.

The doctrine of karma implies that souls are reborn as animals because of past misdeeds. Being reborn as an animal is a serious spiritual setback. Some earlier Buddhist mistakenly thought this met animals are lesser than humans and entitled to fewer rights than human beings, and justified exploitation and mistreatment of animals.

What Buddha taught was to do no harm to animals, or little as possible for protection. To show loving kindness to all beings. The doctrine of right livelihood teaches Buddhists to avoid any work connected with the killing of animals. The doctrine of karma teaches that any wrong behavior will have to be paid for in a future life - so cruel acts to animals should be avoided. Buddhists treat the lives of human and non-human animals with equal respect. Buddhists believe that is wrong to hurt or kill animals, because all beings are afraid of injury and death:

All living things fear being beaten with clubs.
All living things fear being put to death.
Putting oneself in the place of the other,
Let no one kill nor cause another to kill.
Dhammapada 129

We as human beings also have an animal nature that we are blind too. Being blind to it can cause a lot of unnecessary stress. How many times have we did something and we have no idea why. We even said we won't do something again, and we do it anyway, as if we lost all control of our actions. That is because we are blind to our animal nature. Here is a sutra about blind turtle that has as much chance of sticking its head through a hole in a moving yoke as much chance we do to control our behavior when we are blind to our animal nature.

SN 56.48 Chiggala Sutta: The Hole

"Monks, suppose that this great earth were totally covered with water, and a man were to toss a yoke with a single hole there. A wind from the east would push it west, a wind from the west would push it east. A wind from the north would push it south, a wind from the south would push it north. And suppose a blind sea-turtle were there. It would come to the surface once every one hundred years. Now what do you think: would that blind sea-turtle, coming to the surface once every one hundred years, stick his neck into the yoke with a single hole?"

"It would be a sheer coincidence, lord, that the blind sea-turtle, coming to the surface once every one hundred years, would stick his neck into the yoke with a single hole."

"It's likewise a sheer coincidence that one obtains the human state. It's likewise a sheer coincidence that a Tathagata, worthy & rightly self-awakened, arises in the world. It's likewise a sheer coincidence that a doctrine & discipline expounded by a Tathagata appears in the world. Now, this human state has been obtained. A Tathagata, worthy & rightly self-awakened, has arisen in the world. A doctrine & discipline expounded by a Tathagata appears in the world.

"Therefore your duty is the contemplation, 'This is stress... This is the origination of stress... This is the cessation of stress.' Your duty is the contemplation, 'This is the path of practice leading to the cessation of stress.'"

This sutra is a message about how fortunate we are to be humans with self-awareness that we can seek the way of the Buddha. Though when we are blind to our animal instincts we have just as much chance as the blind turtle sticking its head through the hole, which is very rare if any. Therefore through contemplation we can become aware of the animal instincts and not be ruled by them. It is very stressful when one keeps going against their better judgment no matter how hard one seems to try not to.

Therefore by living the noblest lives we can by becoming aware of all aspects of our self.

That includes not letting our animal nature take over where we are a slave to our impulses.

The blindness has a lot to do with social conditioning that causes us to fear parts of our self. Like I said before fear of the unknown reflects a fear of our own self. The monsters created in fiction, symbolizes our own fears about our self.

Many do not know what the human animal is even though we are the human animal. Religious doctrine, mostly of Christianity and Islam which is the Doctrine of Variable Human Worth promotes shame for being a human animal. The doctrine even seeped in the east. That which passes as Christianity first tells us that we are born in sin. From the start we are taught that something inherently is wrong with us that need to be fixed. While we are shamed for having human faults, the God of that religion is said to have those faults as virtues. The double standard is that God is jealous and it's okay, because he's God. God demands worship, God gets angry, God kills those who he pleases. All these characteristics attributed to God are considered virtues, though the bible has to constantly remind people that God is good. The double standard is any human who has any of these characteristics is labeled as a narcissist or psychopath.

Humans have a whole array of emotions and impulses, and for most doctrine shame us for being human. The Doctrine of Variable Worth tells us our worth is based on what we do and what authority dictates what our worth is.

As a human animal we have instincts like all animals for our own survival. As a human animal we have something that is an asset which can also be a liability when it comes to other animals. We are sentient which means we are self-aware. This sometimes gives us advantage or worse than those who walk on all four.

The human animal is a sexual being. The sex drive in the human animal is perhaps stronger than any other animal. We have sex to procreate and to bond through pleasure. It is the drive that moves us to survive through procreation. In the part of the brain called the amygdala causes a fear response when we are in danger. This instinct is so that we can run from danger before our conscious mind can even process what the danger is. This is an asset that causes us to flee danger. The handicap of this instinct is when we have a goal the amygdala causes the flight response which leads to procrastination. This is why so many people won't take actions towards what they want. The side effect is when we don't achieve our needs and wants, we feel hurt which manifests as anger. This would be considered what Buddhism calls violent acts against oneself. This is neglecting what you want in life because of letting fear manifesting as anxiety stop you. Procrastination is a mild subtle form of anxiety. One must face it and push through it.

The human animal also has a survival tribal instinct that is fueled by the desire to want to fit it. This is what causes us to yearn love and attention. When we look within and

123

have unconditional love for our self we do not become desperate for love and attention outside us. Seeking love outside our self is essentially seeking someone else's opinion of you, we tend to respond to loving opinions of others with a corresponding self-opinion of our self.

The more we look outside our self the more attach we are to an idea. The more attached, the more we are in survival mode when that idea is threatened. This boils down to the more attached we are to something, the more dangerous we are.

The human animal is also attracted to the forbidden. When we are told not to do something, it makes us curious. The reason why we are attracted to the forbidden and want what we cannot have is that there is a drive in us towards our awakening toward our true Self which can only be achieved through individual thinking. When we are told we are forbidden to do something, as a natural response we rebel. On the subconscious level we say, "How dare you tell me that I better not do something," it is this subconscious drive that causes us to rebel and go against what we feel is pushed upon us. It is challenging us and we either go into fight or flight mode. The fight response is to want to do what we were told not to do. The flight response is to avoid it with disgust. Sometimes there is the passive aggressive approach which is the fight and flight response. This would be an action seen as disgusting at the same time being drawn to it. The flight response is usually reinforced. It is a learned behavior.

If someone says don't push the red button, we are then tempted to push it. Many times after parents tell their children not to do something, they do it for this reason. It is in us to want what we cannot have. Porn sells because it's in the realm of the forbidden. It would have no power if sex was acceptable as eating a meal. In cultures where everyone walks around naked, it is acceptable and seeing a naked individual doesn't stir arousal like it does in cultures where it is forbidden. Therefore because of this, there is no shame to be attracted to what society has labeled forbidden. In the culture here in the west, doctrine has made humans feel shame for being attracted to the forbidden. Wanting what we cannot have. It is doctrine, abuse or something else that reinforces the flight response where we avoid not to do something we were told. It is learned when we see a taboo as gross, nasty, disgust or dangerous. The flight response is natural when we are facing real danger, outside of that, it is learned behavior.

Shame due to doctrine has made things much worse. Doctrine reinforces that one has committed a sin just by thinking about it. This causes individuals to walk on eggshells and feel guilty for having a passing thought. As human beings we have all kinds of fleeting thoughts throughout the day. We cannot stop those thoughts, most are just fleeting. Thoughts are like catching a bus, if it doesn't apply, let it fly by. Too many times we hop on that thought and ride the thought we do not want because of guilt.

Example: Joe meets his brother's wife for the first time, he looked at her and instantly he recognizes her beauty and may say to himself, "damn she is fine", he acknowledge it as normal reaction and life goes on without another thought about it. In the other scenario, Joe has the same reaction, though due to doctrine that says he committed sin just by that thought he feels guilty for having a normal human response. He says to himself, "I shouldn't have looked at my brother's wife and acknowledged that." Instead of letting it go, he felt guilty and shame for just acknowledging how good his brother's wife is. Due to this, it grows into an obsession where it becomes more than an acknowledgement of her beauty. Now it turns into something else where he felt he had to have her. Before anyone expects it, he is taking actions that he soon began to regret.

The Doctrine of Variable Human Worth is responsible for all kinds of acts of iniquity. It has caused more harm than any good that came from it.

Understanding and accepting the human condition is important. Meditation allows us to go in and have direct inward observation of the human condition. This observation allows us to become more aware of what is going on inside us. When we are more aware of our thoughts, we then can choose those that benefit us and let the useless thoughts pass us by. We are human animals and therefore love yourself unconditionally by accepting all your strengths as well as all your weaknesses.

The animal in us must be tamed, not suppressed. Suppressing the animal is what causes it to ravage and take over. Many who practice spirituality will ignore anything associated with the lower chakras.

When people get caught up in the duality of good versus evil, they are led to believe that the animal instincts are a bad thing. Many people without being grounded in the lower chakras, strive for the higher chakras, to ignore the lower chakras is like trying to build a house on sand. Those instincts reside in the root and sacral chakra, to think what relies there as evil is no different than thinking the roots of all flora is evil.

When any tree grows, it grows equally in both directions. The taller the tree, the deeper its roots, and the health of any tree is determined by its roots. If the roots are unhealthy, then so is the tree. The roots of the tree are the yin (negative polarity) in Chinese philosophy while the tree itself is yang (positive polarity). The Tree is symbolized as the conscious, where the roots is the subconscious. Below is the yin /yang symbol with a tree embedded. (see figure 6).

Figure 6: Tree and Root symbolizing the Conscious and Subconscious

Trees and its roots and nutrients is also an example of cycles and how nothing is actually waste. Decay from dead flesh and feces when in the earth are nutrients for the roots of trees and other foliage. They are not waste, they are fertilizer which is the nutrients to foliage that gives life. Bees pollinate to allow fertilization. Plants provide as plenty of food for herbivores. Carnivores and omnivores eat other omnivores and herbivores. Omnivores eat plants and other omnivores and herbivores. Those animals turn around and poop and eventually die. Decayed flesh that

128

isn't buried is eaten by scavengers. That which is decayed seeps into the earth as with poop becomes nutrients for foliage and the cycle of life starts again. When decay and poop are put in its proper place, it is then nutrients. When our dark impulses are in its proper place, it's healthy for our well-being. When we look outside our self for salvation it is like leaving decay and poop above the earth to poison and stink up the atmosphere. When we look within and love ourselves, then it's like the dead is buried which fertilizer becomes.

Get rid of poop and decay, then the cycle of life stops and all life on this planet dies. If there are no dark impulses within the subconscious, then human have no survival instincts and will die. When we look within and love ourselves then the survival instincts become fertilizer for the roots in the subconscious. Therefore anytime you look outside yourself for salvation, you are stinking up the atmosphere of your conscious mind with decay.

Symbolically, the dead belongs in the earth, not running around upon the surface of the earth bringing hell on earth.

The Bodhi tree that Shakyamuni sat under roots had to be nourished in order for the tree to grow and be healthy. Bodhi means enlightenment, and the leaves on the tree are heart shaped. Even though there are actual Bodhi trees which are sacred fig trees, the one that Gotama sat under until he became the Buddha is symbolic of always being in a meditative state.

Nourishing the roots is to acknowledge the animals instincts while keeping them tamed. Acknowledging them is to honor them.

Die to the philosophy of the masses and honor you animal instincts. Animals such as cats and dogs for example do not worry about the future or dwell on the past. When animals are not starving or in any other discomfort, they are in the eternal present. When you honor those instincts then you are in the present moment with your needs met. When your needs are met, others cannot manipulate you. Your behavior isn't predictable.

When you are in the present moment then you are unpredictable. You take charge in your life and get things done. These are those who learn from their experiences and mastered their world, they do not get stuck in the dark pits of their gloom; instead they rise up and become stronger. When your feet are planted on the ground, you have dominion over your world.

When you are steadfast you have the power to rewrite the script of your life, you have mastery of the flesh. Tantra can stimulate the electrical current in the spine that rises up and has the power to instantly kill ignorance. It is this same unseen power used in mantras and magical ritual, which is the power of intent.

Hell is what we experience when we are unaware of our animal instincts. The three worlds of blindness are concealed within us and drive our subconscious decisions when we don't understand the process of what's going on. When the roots of the Bodhi tree is nourished by honoring those instincts by being in the eternal now then the tree itself will blossom within us.

Chapter 14
The Water Buffalo

Yama and Yamantaka both have the head of the water buffalo. The water buffalo is some traditions symbolizes many things, such as Change, Strength, Service, Dedication, and the Connection to the Earth Mother. Another word for change is death, which is Yama.

Yama as judge of the dead reveals your records and determines your fate. He determines what you will come back as, a human or an animal. Whether you can take this literally or just symbolic, it doesn't matter. Allegorically this is us.

Therefore Yama as judge is symbol of critical thinking, which is about objectively analyzing every situation in order to make a judgment instead of blindly following something. That means not blindly following are animal instincts or what others tell you as their truth.
The bodhisattva Ksitigarbha, is one who shines the light on the dark.

Therefore by definition, symbolically Yama questions the situation, and judges by exposing the crime, while Ksitigarbha shines light on what was concealed by everyone.

Yama is not a conscious being to be worshipped. On the macrocosm and the microcosm Yama is the dark evolutionary force of entropy that permeates all of nature and provides the drive for survival and propagation inherent in all living things.

It is the evolutionary force of entropy that is associated with the 2nd law of thermodynamics. It is energy in motion seeking stillness. Energy is in a constant state of rest, motion and rest. Symbolically, Yamantaka is energy at rest seeking motion while Yama is energy in motion seeking rest, symbolically this is Yamantaka dancing on Yama (Death).

This is not an objective universe, it's a cyclic universe. Objectivity is but one stage of a cycle which is forever moving through many stages between the appearance and disappearance of what the senses interpret as objective.

Therefore Yama symbolizes the polarity of the yin and yang of the universe. Rest seeks motion and motion seeks rest.

Within the root chakra, Yama is a reservoir of power inside each human to be tapped at will.

It's about being our own god. Yama is a symbol of Man living as what his carnal nature dictates, with Yamantaka, that nature is tamed and beneficial. Being grounded in reality one knows that death and pain is a continuing cycle in life, it cannot be escaped. Knowing this, we learn to endure it and accept that it is part of nature. We realize this is reality and therefore to try to escape it as many do is foolish. All we can do is extend our life and live life to the fullest.

There are many realms of the subconscious mind. This realm of animal resides in the root chakra.

Will must be exercise to achieve anything, one must use will to cut through the ignorance, the blindness.

132

This means that you have to be your own god and do what pleases you. This is the path of the bodhisattva. If what you desire pleases you and doesn't hurt you or anyone else, then there is nothing wrong with it.

There is nothing wrong with self-gain. All actions that we do at the core are for our self. There is rational egoism which is also called rational selfishness. The philosopher and author Ayn Rand in her book *The Virtue of Selfishness,* she mentions a rational man holds his own life as his highest value, rationality as his highest virtue, and his happiness as the final purpose of his life. Altruism is the mask one wears to make themselves look good. Altruism is not to be confused with kindness, respect for others or good will. The primary of altruism is the basic absolute of self-sacrifice, self-denial, self-abandonment and self-destruction.

The question is the need for others the first pledge on your life and the moral purpose of your existence? Is man to be regarded as a sacrificial animal? Any man with self-esteem would answer "no", but Altruism says "yes"

Do to our survival mechanism; the behaviors that seem altruistic are actually selfish. When we help others we are also helping ourselves. There is self-gratification when helping another. It makes us feel good. When we see a stranger trapped inside a burning car that is about to catch explode, we rush to help that person even though we may die, because we selfishly couldn't bear to live the rest of our lives knowing that we could have saved someone's life if we tried. We would rather die than to live with such burden of regret. All actions are selfish and there is nothing immoral about rational selfishness.

Altruism is pushed on society by organized religions that say self is bad and selfless is good.

Guilt and shame is pushed on people that seek self-gain. Altruism is used to claim one is good to hide shame while it keeps people blind to what's really going on inside us. It keeps people blind to their animal instincts. As long as we remain blind to them, we are at the mercy of them. It leads to predictable behavior allowing one to be controlled and manipulated by others.

Therefore when being altruistic is mentioned in Buddhism, it is not referring that your moral life is to be a sacrificial animal. One must use common sense, because when it comes down to it, self-preservation comes first.

Liberation is associated with the pineal gland. Through our senses we come to be aware of things around us. Observing the world as an infant we then ask who am I and why am I here. As soon as we do, the ego is born. At that moment we claim an identity. There is nothing wrong with that, it is what is needed in order to survive. The ego only becomes a problem when we put our identity in a box and refuse to expand who we truly are. Keeping our identity boxed up keeps it weak as we continual to seek validation from others and other external things to validate our self-worth.

In the early stage as we seek an identity, we see our mother as god. God is the most important thing or person in one's life. We depend on our mother for survival and in the formative years, everything she says is the word of god, in the infant's eyes. This is a stepping stone, and sadly many do not mature beyond this stage as they just replace other gods in place of their mother.

The formative years are very important to what messages we tell the infant. What that child takes in is an early programming that can dictate that child's destination for the rest of his or her life.

If a mother's message to her child is that they are unloved and do not deserve the good things in life, that child will grow up believing that. There is no good or bad mothers, they are doing the best they know by the capacity they have during that time. Being a mother is a new experience and one can only do with the knowledge and capability they have. I am not condoning a mother who may do horrible things that affect the child; it is that those mothers are ignorant and too narcissistic to even be aware of what they are doing.

One doesn't have to be stuck with the programming from early childhood. We have the knowledge to change that, and that is through meditation.

Life is about taking full personal responsibility for your actions and doing what pleases you without hurting anyone. Doing what gratifies you without relinquishing your responsibility. Doing what makes you happy. You can only be committed to doing what makes you happy. Don't let anyone tell you what's right and wrong. What's wrong for someone else doesn't mean it's wrong for you. Only you can decide.

You must not follow a group which will cause you to give up yourself.

As Yama symbolizing King of the Dead, he teaches magic, necromancy, also knowing the dangerous parts of necromancy to avoid, necromancy is communicating with the dead, especially in order predicting the future. It also involves the allegorical mystery of descending to the land of the dead to gain wisdom. He also teaches legal system, while Yamantaka taught tantra.

In tantra the sex energy can be transformed into Nirvana. It is in this area it can get bogged down with the feelings of guilt and shame that are often associated with sexuality and sexual trauma. It is possible to clear sacral chakra blockages by forgiving yourself and others, and accepting yourself as a sexual being. This is part of being a human animal and its usually repressed with shame and guilt, especially in the west.

The Svadhistana Chakra which is the sacral center is the foundation. It is where our sexual energy resides, it is life, and the opposite would be death. With death there is no foundation, the foundation of the tree is life. Within this foundation is the eternal cycle of life and death. This is the realm of accepting this cycle. Here is where you learn to begin to live life to the fullest without being compulsive.

To have mastery over our lives require understanding what makes us tick. Everything that we want and need in life is there for us. The only thing in the way is our self. Many times our own automatic thoughts get in the way which causes self-sabotaging. Many cannot understand why they just can't get ahead in life. They don't understand why they seem to always hit a brick wall. Many struggle with addictions and don't know why they cannot overcome them, no matter how hard they fight it. It seems to be an endless struggle with very little hope for many.

To have strength is to first have courage. To have courage, one must take risks. The keyword here is action. Fire without Light lives in darkness and one then feels the internal torment of unfulfilled hunger. To have anything in life requires the strength and courage to take action. There is a saying, don't play with scared money. Many times in life we do this in finance and relationships. We lack the spirit to risk the possible of loss. Having spirit has nothing to do with the supernatural; it is having that drive to take action despite the risk.

The element fire has great power in forging the will and determination. The difference between a coward and a hero isn't the lack of fear. Both people experience fear; it is the one with courage who uses the will to face the apparent danger. Risk taking plays a role here. Fire consumes but not without it given back light and warmth. It is passion, desire and power. The fire element is also a symbol of communication and immortality.

One cannot have peace of mind if they are settling for less because they are afraid to lose. We must have courage to gain in life what the universe has provided for all of us. Everything that we need and want is there; the only thing in the way is ourselves. In life we must go into the realm of the unknown. We must invest in life and not just settle for what makes us feel safe.

In order to move forward in life, we must dwell into the unknown. For an addict to become clean and sober, he or she must dwell into the unknown. It is this fear of the unknown that keeps many addicts as slaves of their addiction. Many run back to where they feel safe.

When the root psychological center which is the root chakra is weak, we cannot move past it. We are not grounded which means we are caught up in past regret and future fear. Our whole existence is based on survival at any cost, even if others are hurt.

Like a scorpion is predatory and will sting anything that it feels is a threat, due to its crawling nature close to the ground, it cannot see beyond what's in front of it. Us as individuals when we are in survival mode, we are blinded by what we see in front of us. We then began to feel trapped and in unwanted jobs as we feel we don't have enough of what makes us feel secure. Our emotions are then reactive; where we let our emotions rule us. Being reactive causes us to be impulsive in our behavior.

Letting our emotions rule us is like riding on a wild horse without a saddle and reigns. We will not go where we want to go. The idea is to master our emotions like riding a horse with reigns where we guide the horse to where we want to go.

To do this is through Service. That is by having compassion toward our self by having compassion towards others. This is Service to helping those in need. It is this service toward others takes you out of survival mode.
This is when the emotions (water) are consumed by the red light of Amitābha (fire). The fire of the red light burns away ignorance when we are grounded in the now. This is when we are not dwelling on the past or worried about the future, our desires are purified by being unattached to them.
Service brings a transcendence nature of our emotions. In this state, we are no longer being controlled by our emotions. Like a bird we have the essence of patience with

the ability of flight can see beyond what the crawling animal can see. It can see things from a 'bird's eye view' and don't judge what is only in front of it. This is symbolic of seeing the bigger picture. We are no longer consumed by fear; instead, we see the big picture and can remain calm knowing that things will be okay as long as we are grounded.

When we are grounded then we can understand what it means to love. To love is to be the essence of love, that is by seeing through the eyes of love. Love shares by expanding. Love is light and light expands. Walk into a darkened room and light a candle, the light expands and illuminates the room. Therefore be like the light and see how you can be of service to others.

To have mastery over our lives require understanding what makes us tick. Everything that we want and need in life is there for us. The only thing in the way is our self. Many times our own automatic thoughts get in the way which causes self-sabotaging.

As I said the only thing that gets in our way of enlightenment is our self. To have some mastery and stop getting in our own way is through Dedication. Dedication is the other trait of the water buffalo.

Dedication is Dharma method of "dedication of merit" which allows us to share all the blessings, all the merit and goodness that we have earned. We can send out all the benefits that would otherwise accrue to ourselves, to every living being in the world. It is to send out the goodness with your mind. The power of a concentrated mind for goodness, amplified by the community in unison, makes the connection effective.

The spirit of giving sends the gift, the prayer for well-being, throughout the world, to all creatures, as far as our minds extend. The "dedication of merit' can lead to many positive outcomes, such as a better next life, or a good long life, or as the seed of enlightenment. In the dedication prayer, we are asking that the good merit generated from our practice be directed specifically to enlightenment for all beings.

Here is one of the dedication prayers:

Nagarjuna's Dedication of Merit Prayer
Sonam diyi tamchay zigpa nyi
Tobne nyepay dranam pam chenay
Kye ga na chi balap drukpa yi
Sipay tsole drowa drolpar sho
By this merit may all attain omniscience.
May it defeat the enemy, wrongdoing.
From the stormy waves of birth, old age, sickness and death;
From the ocean of samsara, may I free all beings!

Our connection to the earth is that we are worthy. The earth is the witness that we are all worthy, just because we are alive.

Doctrine of Variable Human Worth, which teaches that an individual's worth is based on what they do, and that people's worthiness is measured by status and has to be earned.

Doctrine also teaches that it's wrong to love yourself. Therefore doctrine becomes a wedge between love and self, so they never unite but only conditionally expose to each other. Due to this measuring people by their worth, doctrine brings nothing in the end but lifelong shame, unworthiness and feeling of badness or inferiority.

This concept that is mostly accepted here in America society is the root of most human disturbances. It is the direct cause of guilt, anger, depression, shyness, procrastination, underachievement, continuing addiction and a wide range of self-defeating behavior.

The Doctrine of Variable Human Worth makes one dependent of external authorities, especially those who are considered respectable people and gods.

We are all born as unique individuals though we are all equal in rights. Being alive on this earth makes all species equally worthy. The error of the social structure of humanity is arranged in horizontal layers. Each person reaches a degree of level with the development or lack of their natural talents. The principle of the strongest is supported in all levels of society allowing the individual to stand or not. Assistance on all levels is based on barter. Example, banks will only lend money to people who already have money. People assist others when they see it will benefit them. This is harsh reality. It is even in the rest of the animal kingdom. A pack of wolves will routinely single out a weak member for prolonged harassment, always instigated by an alpha wolf and carried out with the frenzied compliance of lower-ranking wolves. According to the renowned naturalist and wolf expert R. D. Lawrence, wolves literally "follow their leader" and turn on their pack members if a high-ranking alpha does so.

Monkeys also react the same way. In an experiment when a monkey failed to gain or show respect, the other monkeys pursuit to abuse him, if that monkey wasn't removed from the group he would have been killed.

As humans, we are animals too. Many organized religions will try to separate mankind from nature and the animal kingdom. When humans show weakness they instigate bullies.

When the alpha male or alpha woman bullies someone, that human aggression is ignited and enflamed once the call to attack has been informed by the leader. One way of beating a bully is to start knowing oneself and one's animal natures.

Even in the concrete jungle it's the same, people generally do not care to help those who are considered weak. Humans and other animals can sense when one lacks confidence. If you are walking by a yapping dog, if you show any fear or apprehension the dog will bark furiously or growl louder.

On the other hand, if you show no fear that dog will most likely backup and direct its anger inwardly or just shut up. That dog can sense weakness or lack of immediately, people also do as well. When approaching anyone, whether it's a woman or man you have your eye on, or business proposition, that other person can sense any weakness that you show. If you are confident and show strength, you have a chance. Show any weakness, most likely you will be rejected or a victim of aggression. Showing weakness or strength is evident to everyone around you.

Those who are trapped in the Doctrine of Variable Human Worth, where worth is dictated by those in authority are the ones who will try to reward the undeserving to have positions of power that they are unqualified for. They will grant someone a position because of blood relations or political or religious party. Many people are in positions which they lack skill in and are only there because of inheritance. When someone who has strength and skill take a position, these people cry about how unfair it is. Also the environment has been damaged by the Christian dominance religion that sees man superior than all other animals with a God given right to do as they will. This superiority complex has been used to justify abuse to animals and the environment. As we all continue to pursuit happiness, the walls of organized religion will continue to topple down as more people increasingly see through their deception.

Since there are many in positions because of who they know or related to, let this serve you. Get to know the in crowd where it can boost your chance even if you are not one of them. By getting to befriend those who are positions and showing strength will aid your chances highly in climbing the corporate ladder.

As I said, there are no absolutes of good and evil, you can also take a page from sociopaths. I am not saying become a sociopath. There are many sociopaths in high positions in all walks of life, now why is this? Sociopaths do not compromise and they do not show the weakness of lack of confidence. Sociopaths do not fear rejection and don't care what others may think about them. These are the traits that cause sociopaths to raise into almost any position they desire. The downfall of sociopaths is that they are so narcissistic that they lack empathy. A sociopath has a defective emotional disorder that prevents him from feeling empathy.

Empathy allows one to know what others need, a sociopath lacks in that area, which in turn cause others to feel cheated. Because they lack empathy and cannot give others what they need, they are leeches, for their parasitical nature is in everything they do.

Therefore have empathy and compassion, just don't compromise and have concern what others may think about you. Empathy, not sympathy, empathy is to feel and relate to the needs and pain of others, but not shares the same degree as one may feel as sympathy would. Example is if you are playing a sport and your team wins, you can feel empathy of how the losing team feels. To feel sympathy is to feel the same degree of pain as the team that lost, which would be foolish. In any competitive game or venture if you are having sympathy for your competitors you will hesitate to do what you can to win, because you are too concern that the ones you're competing against will be hurt. It is unhealthy to lesson your chances of success because you feel guilty to succeed because others are not. Your competitors most likely are not going to care how you feel when they win against you, why care how they feel? Many people who have been indoctrinated with this Doctrine of Variable Human Worth don't feel worthy to have happiness. They feel when they are happy and others around them are not, they become overwhelmed with guilt and shame and are willing to sacrifice their own happiness for others.

There are others who compromise because they struggle to say "no" to others, also due to being indoctrinated. I myself struggled with this myself. Having this sympathy is a mask of not feeling as if you yourself are worthy to have happiness. It is shame pretending to be sympathy when it's actually shame due to either fear of rejection or fear of failure. The outcome expresses itself as anger and resentment.

Being too kind by compromising yourself to please others while neglecting what you want, will get you nowhere. It is about balance. A sociopath is unbalanced and so is a people pleaser. It's two opposite extremes. The key is balanced. The "Middle Path" is the balance between two opposites, which is refusing to compromise, not caring what others think of you and having empathy towards others.

As long as you allow yourself to fully enjoy the pleasures of your desires while adhering to reality with sound judgment then you shall rise to any height that you desire.

Doing what gives you pleasure without hurting others raises your vitality. It is this vital existence that gives you more energy to get things done.

These are the traits of the water buffalo which I briefly covered here which is Change, Strength, Service, Dedication, and the Connection to the Earth Mother.

As I mentioned there are mantras to help initiate this, there are also tantra that will also transform us.

Chapter 15
Wheel of Sharp Weapons

The Wheel of Sharp Weapons is a Mahayana Training of the Mind. Symbolically the wheel of Sharp weapons Effectively Striking the Heart of the foe' is often a text referenced as a detailed source for how the laws of karma play out in our lives; it reveals many specific effects and their causes. It was written by the great Yogi Dharmaraksita in his retreat in the jungle where many fierce animals pray. What this great yogi wrote who possessed great knowledge, the full powers of profound insight and logic. What was written was the essence of the teachings of all his Gurus. He has always practiced in accordance with this teaching in his fearsome jungle retreat during the degenerate age in which he lived. Dharmaraksita transmitted these teachings to many disciples and one of them named Atisa (982- 1054) practiced them wherever he went in order to tame those who ware most wild. . Atisa was instrumental in establishing a second wave of Buddhism in Tibet.

When Atisa developed true insight into the Bodhicittas through these teachings, he composed some verses.

I went through much hardship abandoning royalty,
But by collecting much virtuous merit,
I met my true Guru, Dharmaraksita,
By showing me these supreme nectar like teachings,
He has granted me sovereignty over my mind;
So that now I have attained all the forceful opponents,

Having memorised fully these words he has taught.
Although I do not favour a partisan viewpoint-
Whenever I study the various teachings
I always make effort to broaden my wisdom
To see boundless wonders in every tradition-
Yet I have to admit that these teachings especially
Have been of great help in this age of decay.

The Bodhicitta is a spontaneous wish to attain enlightenment motivated by great compassion for all sentient beings, accompanied by a falling away of the attachment to the illusion of an inherently existing self.

The "wheel of sharp weapons" can be visualized as something we throw out or propel, which then comes back to cut us... something like a boomerang. In the same way, Dharmarakṣita explains, the non-virtuous causes we create through our self-cherishing behavior come back to 'cut us' in future lives as the ripening of the negative karma such actions create. This, he explains, is the source of all our pain and suffering. He admonishes that it is our own selfishness or self-cherishing that leads us to harm others, which in turn creates the negative karma or potential for future suffering. Our suffering is not a punishment, merely a self-created karmic result.

In most verses he had suggested alternative virtuous or positive action to substitute for bad behavior in order to create positive karma.

Among his many great disciples in India and Tibet, Atisa transmitted these teachings to Upasaka hBrom-ston-pa, {22} who had been prophesied to be his most fitting disciple by many of Atisa's meditational deities such as Tara. Atisa transmitted these teachings to hBrom-ston-pa in order to pacify the minds of the disciples of remote Tibet who were difficult to tame.

Here are the verses of the Wheel of Sharp Weapons:

The name of this work is 'The Wheel of Sharp Weapons Effectively Striking the Heart of the Foe'.
I pray heartfelt homage to you, Yamantaka;
Your wrath is opposed to the Great Lord of Death.

1) In jungles of poisonous plants strut the peacocks,
Though medicine gardens of beauty lie near.
The masses of peacocks do not find gardens pleasant,
But thrive on the essence of poisonous plants.

2) In similar fashion the brave Bodhisattvas
Remain in the jungle of worldly concern.
No matter how joyful this world's pleasure gardens,
These Brave Ones are never attracted to pleasures,
But thrive in the jungle of suffering and pain.

3) We spend our whole life in the march for enjoyment,
Yet tremble with fear at the mere thought pain;
Thus since we are cowards, we are miserable still.
But the brave Bodhisattvas accept suffering gladly
And gain from their courage a true lasting joy.

4) Now desire is the jungle of poisonous plants here.
Only Brave Ones, like peacocks, can thrive on such fare,
If cowardly beings, like crows, were to try it,
Because they are greedy they might lose their lives.

148

5) How can someone who cherishes self more than others
Take lust and such dangerous poisons for food?
If he tried like a crow to use other delusions,
He would probably forfeit his chance for release.

(6) And thus Bodhisattvas are likened to peacocks:
They live on delusions poisonous plants.
Transforming them into the essence of practice,
They thrive the jungle of everyday life.
Whatever is presented they always accept
While destroying the poison of clinging desire.

(7) Uncontrollable wandering through rounds of existence
Is concern by our grasping at egos as real.
This ignorant attitude heralds the demon
Of selfish concern for our welfare alone:
We seek some security for our own egos;
We want only pleasure and shun any pain.
But now we must banish all selfish compulsion
And gladly take hardship for all other's sake.

(8) All of our sufferings derive from our habits
Of selfish delusions we heed and act out
As all of us share in this tragic misfortune,
Which stems from our narrow and self-centered ways,
We must take all our sufferings and the miseries of others
And smother our wishes of selfish concern.

(9) Should the impulse arise now to seek our own pleasure,
We must turn it aside to please others instead;
For even if loved ones should rise up against us,
We must blame our self-interest and feel it's our due.

(10) When our bodies are aching and racked with great
torment

Of dreadful diseases we cannot endure,
This is the wheel of sharp weapons returning
Full circle upon us from wrongs we have done.
Till now we have injured the bodies of others;
Hereafter let's take on what sickness is theirs.

(11) Depressed and forlorn, when we feel mental anguish,
This is the wheel of sharp weapons returning
Full circle upon us from wrongs we have done.
Till now we how deeply disturbed minds of others;
Hereafter let's take on this suffering ourselves.

(12) When hunger or violent thirst overwhelms us,
This is the wheel of sharp weapons returning
Full circle upon us from wrongs we have done.
Till now we have kept what we had without sharing;
We have plundered end stolen and lured people on.
Hereafter let's take from them hunger and thirst.

(13) When we lack any freedom, but must obey others,
This is the wheel of sharp weapons returning
Full circle upon us from wrongs we have done.
Till now we have looked down upon them who were
lowly
And used them as servants for our own selfish needs;
Hereafter let's offer our service to others
With humble devotion of body and life.

(14) When we hear only language that is foul and abusive,
This is the wheel of sharp weapons returning
Full circle upon us from wrongs we have done.
Till now we have said many things without thinking;
We have slandered and caused many friendships to and.
Hereafter let's censure all thoughtless remarks.

(15) When we are born in oppressive and wretched
condition,
This is the wheel of sharp weapons returning
Full circle upon us from wrongs we have done.
Till now we have always had a negative outlook
We have criticized others, seeing only their flaws
Hereafter let's cultivate positive feelings
And view our surroundings as stainless and pure.

(16) When we are parted from friends and from those
who can help us,
This is the wheel of sharp weapons returning
Full circle upon us from wrongs we have done.
Till now we have taken the friends and good servants
Of others away, wanting them for ourselves;
Hereafter let's never cause close friends to part.

(17) When supreme holy Gurus find us displeasing,
This is the wheel of sharp weapons returning
Full circle upon us from wrongs we have done.
Till now we have turned from the Gurus and teachings,
preferring the counsel of misleading friends;
Hereafter let's end our dependent relations
With those who would turn us away from the path.

(18) When unjustly we are blamed for the misdeeds of
others,
And are falsely accused of flaws that we lack,
And are always the object of verbal abuse,
This is the wheel of sharp weapons returning
Full circle upon us from wrongs we have done.
Till now we have despised and belittled our Gurus;
Hereafter let's never accuse others falsely,
But give them full credit for virtues they have.

(19) When the things we require for daily consumption
And use, fall apart or are wasted or spoil,
This is the wheel of sharp weapons returning
Full circle upon us from wrongs we have done.
Till now we have been careless with others' possessions;
Hereafter let's give them whatever they need.

(20) When our minds are unclear and our hearts are
unhappy,
We are bored doing virtue but excited by vice,
This is the wheel of sharp weapons returning
Full circle upon us from wrongs we have done.
Till now we have led others to acts of non-virtue;
Hereafter let's never provide the conditions
That rouse them to follow their negative traits.

(21) When our minds are disturbed and we feel great
frustration
That things never happen the may that we wish,
This is the wheel of sharp weapons returning
Full circle upon us from wrongs we have done.
Till now we have caused interfering disturbance
When others were focused on virtuous acts;
Hereafter let's stop causing such interruption.

(22) When nothing we do ever pleases our Gurus,
This is the wheel of sharp weapons returning
Full circle upon us from wrongs we have done.
Till now with our Gurus we have feigned pious manners,
But out of their presence have reverted to sin.
Hereafter let's try to be less hypocritical
And take all the teachings sincerely to heart.

(23) When others find fault with whatever we are doing
And people seem eager to blame only us,

This is the wheel of sharp weapons returning
Full circle upon us from wrongs we have done.
Till now we have been shameless, not cared about others,
We have thought that our deeds did not matter at all,
Hereafter let's stop our offensive behavior.

(24) When our servants and friends are annoyed by our habits,
And after a while cannot stay in our homes,
This is the wheel of sharp weapons returning
Full circle upon us from wrongs we have done
Till now we have imposed our bad habits on others;
Hereafter let's change and show only hind ways.

(25) When all who are close turn against us as enemies,
This is the wheel of sharp weapons returning
Full circle upon us from wrongs we have done.
Till now we have held grudges inside us with anger
With thoughts of sly methods to cause others pain;
Hereafter let's try to have less affectation,
Not pretend to be kind while we harbour base aims.

(26) When we suffer from sickness and such interference
Especially when gout has swollen our legs,
This is the wheel of sharp weapons returning
Full circle upon us from wrongs we have done.
Till now without shame and with no self-control
We have stolen or misused what others have given;
Hereafter let's never take anything offered
To the Three Jewels of Refuge as if it were ours.

(27) When strokes and diseases strike without warning,
This is the wheel of sharp weapons returning
Full circle upon us from wrongs we have done.

Till now we have broken our vowed words of honour;
Hereafter let's shun such non-virtuous deeds.

(28) When our mind becomes clouded whenever we
study,
This is the wheal of sharp weapons returning
Full circle upon us from wrongs we have done.
Till now we have thought that the study of Dharma
Lacked prime importance and could be ignored;
Hereafter let's build up the habits of wisdom
To hear and to think about whet Buddha taught.

(29) When sleep overwhelms us while practising virtue,
This is the wheel of sharp weapons returning
Full circle upon us from wrongs we have done.
Till now we have gathered the causes for obstacles
Hindering our practice of virtuous acts.
(We have lacked all respect for the scriptural teachings;
We have sat on our books and left texts on the ground.
We have also looked down upon those with deep insight.)
Hereafter for the sake of our practice of Dharma
Let's gladly endure all the hardships we meet.

(30) When our mind wanders greatly and runs towards
delusion,
This is the wheel of sharp weapons returning
Full circle upon from wrongs we have done.
Till now we have neglected to meditate fully
On defects pervading this transient world;
Hereafter let's work to renounce this existence
(And see the impermanent nature of things).

(31) When all our affairs, both religious and worldly,
Run into trouble and fall into ruin,
This is the wheel of sharp weapons returning

Full circle upon us from wrongs we have done.
Till now we have felt cause and effect {9} could be slighted;
Hereafter let's practise with patience and strength.

(32) When rites we perform never seem to be fruitful,
This is the wheel of sharp weapons returning
Full circle upon us from wrongs we have done.
Till now we have relied on the gods of this world
Or on unskillful actions to bring us relief;
Hereafter let's turn in another direction
And leave our non-virtuous actions behind.

(33) When none of the wishes we make reach fulfillment,
Although we have made prayers to the Three Precious
Gems,
This is the wheel of sharp weapons returning
Full circle upon us from wrongs we have done.
Till now we have had an imperfect commitment
To Buddha whose teachings deserve complete trust;
Hereafter let's place our exclusive reliance
On Buddha, his teachings and those in his fold.

(34) When prejudice, polio or strokes have us crippled
And external forces or harm rise against us,
This is the wheel of sharp weapons returning
Full circle upon us from wrongs we have done.
Till now we have collected vast stores of non-virtue
By breaking, our vows and offending protectors
In our practice from Guru-devotion to tantra; {10}
Hereafter let's banish all prejudiced views.

(35) When we lack all control over where we must travel
And always must wander like waifs with no home,
This is the wheel of sharp weapons returning
Full circle upon us from wrongs we have done.

Till now we have disturbed holy Gurus and others
And forced them to move from their homer or their seats;
Hereafter let's never cause others disturbance
By evicting them cruelly from where they reside.

(36) When the crops in our fields are continually plagued
By drought floods and hailstones, insects and frost,
This is the wheel of sharp weapons returning
Full circle upon us from wrongs we have done.
Till now we have failed to honour our pledges;
Hereafter let's keep all our moral vows pure,

(37) When we are poor, yet are filled with much greed
and desire,
This is the wheel of sharp weapons returning
Full circle upon us from wrongs we have done,
Till now we have been misers, reluctant to share.
The offerings we have made to the Three Jewels were
meager;
Hereafter let's give with a generous hart.

(38) When our bodies are ugly and others torment us
By mocking our flaws, never showing aspect
This is the wheel of sharp weapons returning
Full circle upon us from wrongs we have done.
Till now we have made images lacking in beauty,
By venting our anger we have made ugly scenes;
Hereafter let's print books and make pleasing statues,
And not be short-tempered but be of good cheer.

(39) When attachment and anger disturb and upset us
No matter how much we may try to suppress them,
This is the wheel of sharp weapons returning
Full circle upon us from wrongs we have done.
Till now we have held on to the improper outlook:

Stubbornly cherishing only ourselves,
Hereafter let's uproot self-interest completely.

(40) When success in our practices always eludes us,
This is the wheel of sharp weapons returning
Full circle upon us from wrongs we have done.
Till now, deep within, we have clung to our ego,
Fully immersed in self-cherishing ways;
Hereafter let's dedicate all of the virtuous
Actions we do, so that others may thrive.

(41) When our mind is untamed though we act with great
virtue,
This is the wheel of sharp weapons returning
Full circle upon us from wrongs we have done.
Till now we have engaged in those worldly ambitions
That aim at success for ourselves in this life;
Hereafter let's work with pure one-pointed effort
To nourish the wish to gain freedom's far shore.

(42) When after we do any virtuous action
We feel deep regret or we doubt its effect,
This is the wheel of sharp weapons returning
Full circle upon us from wrongs we have done.
Till now we have been fickle and, stirred by base motives,
Have courted only those who had power or wealth;
Hereafter let's act with complete self-awareness,
Exerting great care in the way we make friends.

(43) When those with ambition repay trusting friendship
By luring us on with their devious schemes,
This is the wheel of sharp weapons returning
Full circle upon us from wrongs we have done.
Till now from ambition we have acted with arrogance,
Hereafter let's dampen our self-centered pride.

(44) When the force of attraction or that of repulsion
Colours whatever we hear or we say,
This is the wheel of sharp weapons returning
Full circle upon us from wrongs we have done.
Till now we have ignored what has caused all our troubles:
The mass of delusion that dwells in our heart;
Hereafter let's try to abandon all hindrances
Note their arisal, examine them wed.

(45) When no matter how well-meant our actions
towards others,
They always elicit a hostile response,
This is the wheel of sharp weapons returning
Full circle upon us from wrongs we have done.
Till now we have repaid loving-kindness with malice;
Hereafter let's always accept others' favours
Both graciously and with most humble respect.

(46) In short then, whenever unfortunate suffering
We haven't desired crash upon us like thunder,
This is the same as the smith who had taken
His life with a sword he had fashioned himself
Our suffering is the wheel of sharp weapons returning
Full circle upon us from wrong we have done.
Hereafter let's always have care and awareness
Never to act in non-virtuous ways.

(47) All of the sufferings that we have endured
In the lives we have led in the three lower states,
As well as our pains of the present and future,
Are the same as the case of the forger of arrows
Who later was killed by an arrow he had made.
Our suffering is the wheel of sharp weapons returning
Full circle upon us from wrong we have done.

Hereafter let's always have care and awareness
Never to act in non-virtuous ways.

(48) When the troubles and worries of family life grieve
us,
This is the same as the case of a child
Who was cared for with love later killing his parents.
Our suffering is the wheel of sharp weapons returning
Full circle upon us from wrong we have done.
Hereafter it is fitting in all of our lifetimes
For us to live purely as monks or as nuns.

(49) As it's true what I have said about self-centered
interest,
I recognize clearly my enemy now.
I recognize clearly the bandit who plunders,
The liar who lures by pretending he is part of me;
Oh what relief that I have conquered this doubt!

(50) And so Yamantaka spin round with great power
The wheel of sharp weapons of good actions now.
Three times turn it round, in your wrathful-like aspect-
Your legs set apart for the two grader of truth,
With your eyes blazing open for wisdom and means.

(51) Baring your fangs of the four great opponents,
Devour the foe-our cruel selfish concern!
With your powerful mantra of cherishing others,
Demolish this enemy lurking within!

(52) Frantically running through life's tangled jungle,
We are chased by sharp weapons of wrongs we have done
Returning upon us; we are out of control
This sly, deadly villain-the selfishness in us,
Deceiving ourselves and all others a well-

Capture him, capture him, fierce Yamantaka,
Summon this enemy, bring him forth now!

(53) Batter him, batter him, rip out the heart
Of our grasping for ego, our love for ourselves!
Trample him, trample him, dance on the head
Of this treacherous concept of selfish concern!
Tear out the heart of this self-centered butcher
Who slaughters our chance to gain final release!

(54) Hum! Ham! Show all your powers, O mighty
protector.
Dza! Dza! Tie up this enemy; do not let him loose.
P'a! P'a! {17} Set us free by your might, O great Lord over
Death
Cut! Cut! Break the knot of self-interest that binds us
inside.

(55) Appear Yamantaka, O wrathful protector;
I have further entreaties to make of you still.
This sack of five poisons, mistakes and delusions,
Drags us down in the quicksand of life's daily toil—
Cut it off, cut it off, rip it to shreds!

(56) We are drawn to the sufferings of miserable rebirths,
Yet mindless of pain, we go after its cause.
Trample him, trample him, dance on the head
Of this treacherous concept of selfish concern,
Tear out the heart of this self-centered butcher
Who slaughters our chance to gain final release.

(57) We have high expectations of speedy attainments,
Yet do not wish to work at the practice involved.
We have many fine projects we plan to accomplish,
Yet none of them ever are done in the end.

160

Trample him, trample him, dance on the head
Of this treacherous concept of selfish concern,
Tear out the heart of this self-centered butcher
Who slaughters our chance to gain final release.

(58) Our wish to be happy is strong at all times,
Yet we do not gather merit to yield this result.
We have little endurance for hardship and suffering,
Yet ruthlessly push for the things we desire.
Trample him, trample him, dance on the head
Of this treacherous concept of selfish concern,
Tear out the heart of this self-centered butcher
Who slaughters our chance to gain final release.

(59) With comparative ease, we develop new friendships,
Yet since we are callous, not one of them lasts.
We are filled with desire for food and fine clothing,
Yet failing to earn them, we steal and we scheme.
Trample him, trample him, dance on the head
Of this treacherous concept of selfish concern,
Tear out the heart of this self-centered butcher
Who slaughters our chance to gain final release.

(60) We are experts as flattering others for favours,
Yet always complaining, we are sad and depressed.
The money we have gathered we cannot bear to part with;
Like misers we hoard it and feel we are poor.
Trample him, trample him, dance on the head
Of this treacherous concept of selfish concern,
Tear out the heart of this self-centered butcher
Who slaughters our chance to gain final release.

(61) We have done very little to benefit someone,
Yet always remind him how much we have done.
We have never accomplished a thing in our lifetime,

Yet boasting and bragging, we are filled with conceit.
Trample him, trample him, dance on the head
Of this treacherous concept of selfish concern,
Tear out the heart of this self-centered butcher
Who slaughters our chance to gain final release.

(62) We have many great masters and teachers to guide us
Yet shirking our duty, ignore what they teach.
We have many disciples, yet do not met help them;
We cannot be bothered to give that advice.
Trample him, trample him, dance on the head
Of this treacherous concept of selfish concern,
Tear out the heart of this self-centered butcher
Who slaughters our chance to gain final release.

(63) We promise to do many glorious dads,
Yet In practice we give others minimal help.
Our spiritual fame has been spread far and wide,
Yet inwardly all of our thoughts are repulsive
Not only to gods, but to demons and ghosts.
Trample him, trample him, dance on the head
Of this treacherous concept of selfish concern,
Tear out the heart of this self-centered butcher
Who slaughters our chance to gain final release.

(64) We have read very little, heard only few teachings,
Yet talk with authority pertly on Voidness.
Our knowledge of scriptures is pitifully lacking,
Yet glibly we make up and say what we like.
Trample him, trample him, dance on the head
Of this treacherous concept of selfish concern,
Tear out the heart of this self-centered butcher
Who slaughters our chance to gain final release.

(65) We have many attendants and people around us,
Yet no one obeys us or heeds what we say.
We feel we have friends in positions of power,
Yet should we need help, we are left on our own.
Trample him, trample him, dance on the head
Of this treacherous concept of selfish concern,
Tear out the heart of this self-centered butcher
Who slaughters our chance to gain final release.

(66) We have gained lofty status and ranks of prestige.
Yet our knowledge is poorer than that of a ghost.
We are considered great Gurus, yet even the demons
Do not harbour such hatred or clinging desire
Or as closed-minded an outlook-as we seem to have.
Trample him, trample him, dance on the head
Of this treacherous concept of selfish concern,
Tear out the heart of this self-centered butcher
Who slaughters our chance to gain final release.

(67) We talk about theories and the most advanced
teachings,
Yet our everyday conduct is worse than a dog's.
We are learned, intelligent, versed in great knowledge,
Yet cast to the Wind wisdom's ethical base.
Trample him, trample him, dance on the head
Of this treacherous concept of selfish concern,
Tear out the heart of this self-centered butcher
Who slaughters our chance to gain final release.

(68) We have selfish desires and horrible anger,
Which fester inside us, we would never admit;
Yet without provocation we criticize others
And self-righteously charge them with faults we possess.
Trample him, trample him, dance on the head
Of this treacherous concept of selfish concern,

163

Tear out the heart of this self-centered butcher
Who slaughters our chance to gain final release.

(69) We wear robes of saffron, yet seek our protection
And refuge in spirits and gods of this world.
We have promised to keep solemn vows of strict morals,
Yet our actions accord with the demons, foul ways.
Trample him, trample him, dance on the head
Of this treacherous concept of selfish concern,
Tear out the heart of this self-centered butcher
Who slaughters our chance to gain final release.

(70) Our pleasure and happiness come from the Buddhas,
The Gurus, the teachings, and those who live by them,
Yet still we make offerings to ghosts and the spirits.
All of our guidance derives from the teachings,
And yet we deceive those who give this advice.
Trample him, trample him, dance on the head
Of this treacherous concept of selfish concern,
Tear out the heart of this self-centered butcher
Who slaughters our chance to gain final release.

(71) We seek to have homes in monastic seclusion,
Yet dawn by distractions, we venture to town.
Discourses we hear teach us most noble practice,
Yet we spend all our time telling fortunes with dice.
Trample him, trample him, dance on the head
Of this treacherous concept of selfish concern,
Tear out the heart of this self-centered butcher
Who slaughters our chance to gain final release.

(72) We give up monks' vows, the true path to gain
freedom,
We would rather be married, have children and homes.
We cast to-the wind this rare chance to be happy,

And pursue further suffering, mare problems and woes
rample him, trample him, dance on the head
Of this treacherous concept of selfish concern,
Tear out the heart of this self-centered butcher
Who slaughters our chance to gain final release.

(73) Discarding our practice to reach Liberation,
We drift about searching for pleasure or trade.
We have obtained bodies with precious endowments,
Yet use them to gain only hellish rebirths.
Trample him, trample him, dance on the head
Of this treacherous concept of selfish concern,
Tear out the heart of this self-centered butcher
Who slaughters our chance to gain final release.

(74) Ignoring effects that the teachings can bring us,
We travel on business for profit end gain.
Leaving behind all our Gurus' wise lectures,
We tour different places in search of some fun.
Trample him, trample him, dance on the head
Of this treacherous concept of selfish concern,
Tear out the heart of this self-centered butcher
Who slaughters our chance to gain final release.

75) We hoard whet we have, never willing to use it,
And leech all our food and our clothing from friends.
We leave aside wealth from our father's inheritance,
Taking from others a much as we can.
Trample him, trample him, dance on the head
Of this treacherous concept of selfish concern,
Tear out the heart of this self-centered butcher
Who slaughters our chance to gain final release.

(76) It's amazing how little endurance we have
To do meditation, and yet we pretend

To have gained special powers so others are fooled.
We never catch up with the paths of deep wisdom,
Yet run here and there in a needless great haste.
Trample him, trample him, dance on the head
Of this treacherous concept of selfish concern,
Tear out the heart of this self-centered butcher
Who slaughters our chance to gain final release.

(77) Someone giver us advice from the depths of his heart,
Which is for our own good, but is harsh to our ears,
And with anger we view him as if he is our foe.
Yet when someone without any true feelings for us
Deceitfully tells us what we like to hear,
Without taste or discernment we are hind in return.
Trample him, trample him, dance on the head
Of this treacherous concept of selfish concern,
Tear out the heart of this self-centered butcher
Who slaughters our chance to gain final release.

(78) When others consider us close and dear friends
And relate in strict confidence ah they know,
We disclose their deep secrets to especially their foes.
When we have a good friend who is constantly with us,
We locate his weak points so we can torment him.
Trample him, trample him, dance on the head
Of this treacherous concept of selfish concern,
Tear out the heart of this self-centered butcher
Who slaughters our chance to gain final release.

(79) Our jealousy is strong and whatever is said
We are always the sceptic, we doubt what is meant.
We are fussy bad-tempered and hard to get on with,
Inflicting obnoxious behavior on others.
Trample him, trample him, dance on the head
Of this treacherous concept of selfish concern,

Tear out the heart of this self-centered butcher
Who slaughters our chance to gain final release.

(80) When someone requests us to do something for him,
We are never obliging, but think up instead
Clever devious methods to do him some harm.
When others concede and agree with our viewpoint,
We do not acquiesce-we argue still more.
Trample him, trample him, dance on the head
Of this treacherous concept of selfish concern,
Tear out the heart of this self-centered butcher
Who slaughters our chance to gain final release.

(81) We do not pay attention to whet others tell us;
We are a trial to be with; we strain others' nerves.
Our feelings are hurt at the slightest remark,
And we hold grudges strongly-we never forgive.
Trample him, trample him, dance on the head
Of this treacherous concept of selfish concern,
Tear out the heart of this self-centered butcher
Who slaughters our chance to gain final release.

(82) We always are jealous of those of greet status;
We feel holy Gurus ere threats to avoid
Overwhelmed by attachment and ruled by our passions,
We spend all our time lusting after young loves.
Trample him, trample him, dance on the head
Of this treacherous concept of selfish concern,
Tear out the heart of this self-centered butcher
Who slaughters our chance to gain final release.

(83) We do not think of friendships as long-term
commitments
We treat old companions with thoughtless neglect.
And when we are making new friends with a stranger,

167

We try to impress him with grandiose ways.
Trample him, trample him, dance on the head
Of this treacherous concept of selfish concern,
Tear out the heart of this self-centered butcher
Who slaughters our chance to gain final release.

(84) We lack clairvoyance, yet we, feigning powers,
And then when proved wrong, we must bar all
complaints.
We have little compassion for those who are near us,
Whenever they blunder, we are quick to lash out
Trample him, trample him, dance on the head
Of this treacherous concept of selfish concern,
Tear out the heart of this self-centered butcher
Who slaughters our chance to gain final release.

(85) We have poor education and limited knowledge;
Whenever we speak we are unsure of ourselves.
Our learning in scriptural texts is so meagre,
When hearing new teachings we doubt they are true
Trample him, trample him, dance on the head
Of this treacherous concept of selfish concern,
Tear out the heart of this self-centered butcher
Who slaughters our chance to gain final release.

(86) By making a habit of anger and passion,
We come to despise everyone that we meet
And by making a habit of jealous resentment,
We ascribe fruits to others, disclaiming their worth.
Trample him, trample him, dance on the head
Of this treacherous concept of selfish concern,
Tear out the heart of this self-centered butcher
Who slaughters our chance to gain final release.

(87) We do not follow proper Procedures of study;
We say it is needless to read the vast texts.
We feel there is no value learning from Gurus;
We slight oral teachings and think we know best.
Trample him, trample him, dance on the head
Of this treacherous concept of selfish concern,
Tear out the heart of this self-centered butcher
Who slaughters our chance to gain final release.

(88) We fail to explain what the 'Three Baskets teach,
But instead dwell on theories we have made up ourselves.
We lack deep conviction and faith in the teachings,
Whatever we say leaves disciples confused.
Trample him, trample him, dance on the head
Of this treacherous concept of selfish concern,
Tear out the heart of this self-centered butcher
Who slaughters our chance to gain final release.

(89) We do not despise actions unwise and immoral,
Instead we dispute and attempt to pick flaws
In the excellent teachings and great masters' works.
Trample him, trample him, dance on the head
Of this treacherous concept of selfish concern,
Tear out the heart of this self-centered butcher
Who slaughters our chance to gain final release.

(90) We are never embarrassed when acting disgracefully,
Only respectable deeds cause us shame.
Trample him, trample him, dance on the head
Of this treacherous concept of selfish concern,
Tear out the heart of this self-centered butcher
Who slaughters our chance to gain final release.

(91) All the things we should do we do not do even once,
For improper behavior taker up all our time.

Trample him, trample him, dance on the head
Of this treacherous concept of selfish concern,
Tear out the heart of this self-centered butcher
Who slaughters our chance to gain final release.

(92) O mighty destroyer of selfishness demons,
With Body of Wisdom unchained from all bonds,
Yamantaka come brandish your skull-headed bludgeon
Of egoless wisdom of Voidness and bliss.
Without any misgiving now wield your fierce weapon
And wrathfully swing it three times round your head.

(93) With all of your fierceness come smash this foul
enemy!
Burst ego-concepts with your wisdom's great might!
With your boundless compassion protect us from suffering
The miseries caused by our self-centered actions
Destroy our self-cherishing once and for all!

(94) With all the sufferings that others experience,
Smother completely or selfish concern.
The sufferings of others arise from five poisons;
Thus whichever delusion afflicts other beings
Take it to smother delusions self.

(95) Through we have not a doubt, for we recognise fully
The cause and the root of mistakes we all make,
If there is still left a part of our minds that would tend
To support this delusion of self that we have,
Then destroy the firm hold of this part of our minds
That, against or true wishes, makes fools of us still.

(96) As all that is wrong can be traced to one source:
Our concern for ourselves, whom we cherish the most,
We must meditate now on the kindness of others.

Accepting the suffering that they never wished for,
We must dedicate fully our virtues to all.

(97) Thus accepting ourselves all deluded non-virtuous
Actions that others have done in the past,
In the present and future with mind, speech and body,
May delusions of others as well as our own
Be the favoured conditions to gain our Enlightenment
Just as the peacocks eat poison and thrive.

(98) As crows may be cured after swallowing poison
By a powerful antidote given in time,
Let's direct to all others our virtuous merit,
That this may replenish their chances for freedom
May all sentient beings reach Buddhahood soon!

(99) Till the time when all motherly beings and I
Gain the perfect conditions for us to be Buddhas,
Though the force of our actions may cause us to wander
Through various realms in the six rebirth states
May we always be able to help one another
To keep our aim find on Enlightenment's shore.

(100) Then for even the sake of but one sentient being
May we gladly take birth in the three lower states.
With Enlightening Conduct that never grows weak
May we lead al the beings in miserable rebirths
Out of their sufferings and causes for pain.

(101) As soon as we have placed ourselves into their realm
May the guards of the hells come to see us as Gurus,
May the weapons of torture they hold turn to flowers;
May all harm be stilled-peace and happiness grow.

171

(102) Then may even hell beings develop clairvoyance
And take higher rebirths as men or as gods.
By developing strongly the wish to be Buddhas,
May they pay back our kindness through heeding the
teachings
And regard us as Gurus with confident true.

(103) Then may ah sentient beings of the three higher
rebirths
Perfect meditation on Egolessness
In this way may they realise the non-self-existence
Of worldly involvement and freedom as well.
May they place concentration on both of these equally,
Seeing their natures as equally void.

(104) If we practise these methods we shall soon overcome
Our true enemies: selfish concern and self-love.
If we practise their methods we shall overcome also
false concepts of ego we hold to be real
Thus by joint meditation on Egolessness
And on non-dual wisdom of Voidness and Bliss,
How can anyone not gain the causes to win
A Buddha's Physical Body and its fruit, Buddhahood

(105) O mind, understand that the topics discussed here
Are interdependent phenomena all;
For things must rely on dependent-arising
To have an existence-they cannot stand alone,
The process of change is alluring like magic,
For physical form is but mental appearance,
As a torch whirling round seems a circle of flame.

(106) There is nothing substantial to anyone's life-force
It crumbles apart like a water-soaked log
And there is nothing substantial to anyone's life-span

It bursts in an instant like bubbles of foam.
All the things of this world are but fog-like appearance;
When closely examined, they out of sight.
Like mirages these things at a distance seem lovely
But when we come closer, they are not to be found.

(107) All things are like images found in a mirror,
And yet we imagine they are real, very real;
All things are like mist or like clouds on a mountain,
And yet we imagine they are stable and firm.
Our foe: our insistence on ego-identities
Truly our own, which we wish were secure,
And our butcher: the selfish concern for ourselves
Like all things there appear to be truly existent,
Though they never have been truly existent at all.

(108) Although they appear to be concrete and real,
They have never been real, any time, anywhere.
They are not things we should burden with ultimate value,
Nor should we deny them their relative truth.
As our grasping for egos and love for ourselves
Lack substantial foundations with true independence,
How can they yield acts that exist by themselves?
And then how can this cruel vicious circle of suffering,
The fruit of these actions, be real from its core?

(109) Although all things thus lack inherent existence,
Yet just as the face of the moon can be seen
In a cup of clear water reflecting its image,
The various aspects of cause and effect
Appear in this relative world as reflections.
So please, in this world of appearances only,
Let's always be sure what we do is of virtue
And shun all those acts that would cause us great pain.

(110) When our bodies are charred in a horrible nightmare
By the world-ending flames of a stellar explosion,
Although this ordeal is not actually happening
We nevertheless feel great terror and scream.
In similar fashion unfortunate rebirths
In hells or as ghosts are not actually real,
And yet we can fully experience their pain.
Thus fearing such suffering as burning alive,
We must cease all these actions that yield this result.

(111) When our mind are delirious, burning with fever,
Although there is no darkness, we feel we are plummeting
Further and further inside a black pit
With the walls pressing closer the deeper we fall.
In similar fashion, although our dark ignorance
Lacks self-existence, we nevertheless
Must by all means break out of its strangling construction
By putting the three kinds of wisdom to use.

(112) When musicians are playing a beautiful melody,
Should we examine the sound they are making
We would see that it does not exist by itself.
But when we are not making our formal analysis,
Still there is a beautiful tune to be heard,
Which is merely a label on notes and on players
That is why lovely music can lighten sad hearts.

(113) When we closely examine effects and their causes,
We see that they both lack inherent existence
They cannot stand alone, either whole or apart
Yet there seem to exist independently rising
And falling events, which, in fact, are conditioned
By various forces, components and parts,
It is this very level on which we experience
Birth and our death and whatever life brings.

So please, in this world of appearances only,
Let's always be sure what we do is of virtue
And shun all their acts that would cause ns great pain.

(114) When a vase has been filled by the dripping of
water,
The first drops themselves did not fill it alone;
Nor was it made full by the last several drops.
It was filled by an interdependent collection
Of causes and forces that came all together
The water, the pourer, the vase and such things.

(115) It is precisely the same when we come to experience
Pleasure and pain: the results of our past
Effects never come from the first causal actions,
Nor do they arise from the last several acts.
Both pleasure and pain come from interdependent
Collections of forces and causes combined.
So please, in this world of appearances only,
Let's always be sure what we do is of virtue
And shun all their acts that would cause us great pain.

(116) When not making formal dissections with logic,
Merely letting life's happening flow freely on,
Although we experience feelings of pleasure,
In ultimate truth the appearance of happiness
Lacks self-existence inherently real.
And yet on the everyday operative level
This seeming appearance has relative truth.
To understand fully this deep profound meaning
For slow-minded persons, alas, will be hard.

(117) And now when we try to do close contemplation
On Voidness, how can we have even a feeling
Of conventional truth at the very same time?

Yet what can there be that has true self-existence;
And what can there be that lacks relative truth?
How can anyone anywhere believe in such things?

(118) Just as objects of Voidness are non-self-existent,
The Voidness of objects itself is the same.
The shunning of vice and the practice of virtue
Are like wise devoid of all mantel constructions
That they are independent, self-contained acts
In fact, on the whole, they are lacking completely
All mental projections and an pre-conceptions.
Thus if we can focus our clear concentration
On Voidness without our mind wandering astray,
Then truly we shall come to be wondrous beings
With a deep understanding of the most profound Void.

(119) By practising this way the two Bodhicittas,
Of the ultimate and the conventional truth,
And thus by completing without interference
Collections of insight and merit as wall,
May all of us quickly attain Full Enlightenment
Granting what we and all others have wished.

This work has been translated from Sanskrit into
Tibetan by the Atisa himself and his spiritual hBrom-ston-
pa.

This translation of the Tibetan Theg-pa-chen-pohi-blo-
sbyong-mtson-cha-hkhor-lo into English has been prepared
by Geshe Ngawang Dhargyey, Sharpa TulLu, Khamlung
Tulku, Alexander Berzin and Jonathan Landaw at the
Library of Tibetan Works and Archives, at the
Headquarters of His Holiness the Dalai Lama, Dharamsala,
India.

Yamantaka is the wrathful aspect of Manjusri, who is a bodhisattva associated with prajñā (insight). In Tibet he is also called yidam and his name means "Gentle Glory." He is the emanation of the wisdom of the Buddhas.

Yamantaka's wrath is directed against selfishness, self-cherishing attitudes, ego boasting and ignorance. These attitudes take the life of our chance to gain Enlightenment, and thus Yamantaka's wrath is opposed to the Great Lord of Death, Yama.

This is all symbolic of what takes place inside us when we meditate. Yamantaka symbolizes meditation.

Bodhisattvas, or brave Ones, Sons of the Buddhas, are those individuals who have the enlightened Attitude (Bodhicitta) to work towards the attainment of Buddhahood, for the sake of all beings.

There are five points of similarity between Bodhisattvas and peacocks. Just as the colours of the peacocks' feathers grow more radiantly brilliant when they eat plants that may be poisonous to other animals, Bodhisattvas shine with blissful happiness by making use of such poisonous delusions a desire and attachment for the benefit of others. Just as peacocks have five crown feathers, Bodhisattvas have the attainment of the five graded paths for enlightenment. Just as the sight of a peacock's colourful display gives us great pleasure, the sight of a Bodhisattva uplifts our mind because of his Bodhicitta. Just as peacocks live on poisonous plants and never insects or cause others harm, Bodhisattvas never cause even the slightest harm to other sentient beings. Just as peacocks eat poisonous plants with pleasure, when Bodhisattvas are offered objects and enjoy objects and other things, although they have no attachment for these objects, they accept them with pleasure to allow the donor to gain merit from his offering.

There are three levels of training of the mind according to the three levels of motivation outlined in the 'Lam-rim' teaching of the 'Graded Course to Enlightenment'. On the initial level of motivation, we work to attain a better future rebirth. On the intermediate level, we work to attain Liberation (Nirvana) from the vicious circle of rebirth (samsara) for ourselves alone. On the advanced level, as a follower of the Mahayana path, with Bodhicitta motivation we work to attain the enlightenment of Buddhahood for the benefit of all beings.

With the advanced level motivation, there are two ways in which we can follow the Mahayana path. By following the Perfection Vehicle (Paramitayana), it may take many life times before we reach our goal of Enlightenment or following the Tantra Vehicle (Vajrayana), which allows us to attain Enlightenment within one lifetime. The word 'here' in the text indicates the immediacy of practicing the tantra path with an especially strong Bodhicitta motivation.

The tantra system teaches many methods for the quick attainment of Enlightenment. Included among there is the use as a path of the normally poisonous delusions. In order to use delusions, such as lustful desire, as a path, however, we must first be devoid of the self-cherishing attitude, that the greedy attachment to our own self-interest. In addition we must have a sound understanding of Voidness the fact that all things, including ourselves, lack a truly independent manner of existence. To use delusions as a path without these two prerequisites is extremely dangerous and, far from achieving our intended goal, which can cause us to regress.

Any of the delusions may be used in the tantra system as an actual path to Enlightenment. In the Perfection Vehicle, the delusions may only be used as a method for directly benefiting others when the circumstances demand it. They may not, however be practiced as an actual path. To practice as an actual path is missing the mark. The delusions are to be used as a tool, not the focus. Example would be using lustful desire as a tool, instead of the focus.

The Three Jewels of Refuge are the Buddha, his teachings (Dharma), and the monastic community (Sangha) of those who understand end result practice these teachings. The Three Jewels of Refuge are also referred to as the Three Precious Gems or the Triple Gem.

The skull-headed bludgeon of Yamantaka represents the wisdom of emptiness common in both the sutra and tantra traditions. That emptiness is to understand how we are interdependent and that things are not separated from each other. The appearances of forms are all based on the vibration of electromagnetic energy field that is infinitely everywhere. Yamantaka swinging his weapon three times around his head symbolizes the destruction of (1) ego-grasping, (2) our self-cherishing attitude that prevents us from compassionate bodhicitta and achieving enlightenment and (3) our defiled bodies of delusion arising from the two demons which is attachment to desire and ignorance.

The enlightened and fiercely attributes of Yamantaka is shown in his imagery. His deep blue skin color represents clear wisdom as boundless as space. Nine faces symbolizes the nine traditional Buddhist scriptures, thirty four arms, and sixteen legs, large belly and stands on a sun disc with an aura of flames, his erect penis symbolizing great bliss. His face is that of a black buffalo, extremely fearsome with eyebrows, eye lashes and a beard all ablazed and the hair on his head bristling upwards symbolizing attaining nirvana. Instead of the five crowned jewels of the peaceful dieties, he has five skulls adorned around his head symbolizing the five Buddha families and he wears a garland of fifty severed human heads that symbolizes purity of speech, the number fifty represents the number of vowels and consonants in Sanskrit alphabet. His two horns are the two levels of truth. Between the two horns is a fierce red face of Manjushri. On his right are three faces, blue red and yellow. On the left are thre more faces, white, smoked colored and black. Each face has three eyes. The thirty four arms, combined with his body, speech and mind, symbolize the thirty seven limbs of Enlightenment. His uppermost right and left hands holds freshly severed skin of an elephant, stretched open by its left fore and hind legs.

The next two right and left hands at his heart holds a curved knife and skull cup filled with blood. The remaining thirty hands hold different weapons such as axe, spear,

180

bludgeon and sword to destroy illusions and obstacles and a hand drum and bell to make and enjoy offerings.

His eight right feet trample upon a human being, buffalo, bullock, donkey, camel, dog, sheep, and fox. His left feet stand upon a vulture, owl, raven, parrot, hawk, kite, mynah bird and swan.

Also being trampled are the eight celestial devas such s Brahma, Indra, Vishnu, Rudra, six headed Kumara, Ganesh, and the gods of the Sun and Moon.

The sixteen legs are the sixteen kinds of emptiness. The man and animals under his right foot represents the eight great accomplishments. The eight birds under his left foot represent the eight powers and the eight gods, four on each side, which shows that Yamantaka surpasses the glory of the heavenly beings. Being naked means his mind is not covered by any obstructions.

When the practioner visualizes they are Yamantaka and remember all what these symbols stand for, this greatly enhances the confidence that is so important for transformation.

There are many levels of the symbols behind these symbols of death and decay. Yamantaka is one who overcomes Yama, the Lord of Death.

Chapter 16
Guhyasamaja

Western history is different than Indian history, while western history is very linear and based on objective facts and records; Indian view of history is very much mixed with myth, what we would call myth.

Looking at history, it's supposed to illustrate something, teach us something, not just recorded facts. And in terms of tantra and even with Mahayana sutras and so on that have many great masters either receiving direct things from Vajradhara in various manifestations, or Buddha teaching to somebody that then gives it to the nagas and then it's returned, or going up to some heaven and getting teachings from Maitreya, and so on.

Guhyasamaja (gsang-ba 'dus-pa) means "the assembly of hidden or secret factors." Guhya (gsang-ba) means "secret," and samaja ('dus pa) means an "assembly." It is secret as in hidden in nature, it is a form of esoteric Buddhism.

The Guhyasamaja tantra was given by Shakyamuni Buddha to King Indrabhuti who asked the Blessed One, "By what means can people like me who are not detached achieve liberation?," in response Shakyamuni manifested as Guhyasamaja and taught Indrabhuti the highest form of tantra. Tantr involves mantras, meditation, yoga, and ritual. The Sanskrit word Tantra is related to the concept of weaving and expansion- it derives from 'tan', meaning to expand, spin out, and weave. We weave the strands of our nature into a unified whole. Tantra is about embracing the body and desires on the road to enlightenment. One can embrace without being attached.

There is mother tantra and father tantra. Father tantra is "method tantra" and mother tantra as "wisdom sutra."

Tibetan lamas who have taken the name "yoginī tantra" and then created the terms mother tantra and father tantra are in keeping with the Ornament of Vajra Essence Tantra when it says:

The Ornament of Vajra Essence Tantra is the grandmother of all ḍāka mother and ḍāka father tantras.

Division of tantra into two types in keeping with the meanings of the names

1. Points of doubt
2. Individual assertions

Method deals with goal oriented practices such as development of compassion, love, patience, perseverance, etc. on the other hand wisdom focuses on piercing the depths of reality. Method and wisdom are said to be the two wings of the bird that flies to enlightenment.

Two wings are needed because the goal of Buddhahood is twofold which is the consequence and enlightened state known as the dharmakāya, ("wisdom body,") which is the clear knowledge of a Buddha, and the resultant embodiment of that enlightened mind, known as the rūpakāya, ("form body.") The method wing accomplishes the rūpakāya, and that of wisdom accomplishes the dharmakāya.

Figure 7: Thangka of Guhyasamaja in union with his consort Sparshavajrā, 17th century, Rubin Museum of Art

The reality or final truth of all phenomena is not something that came from the Buddha. It is the nature of reality that always existed. The Egyptians knew this, the Sumerians as well as other cultures.

The practices of method in tantra are generally recognized to be superior to those of sutra. This is true in the highest level of tantra, known as highest yoga tantra (anuttarayoga tantra).

The method refers to two unique practices not found in non-tantric Buddhist practices. The method could refer to any state of mind that focuses on the ultimate truth of emptiness, that separation is an illusion. Usually a mind dedicated to the view of emptiness belongs to the wisdom wing of practice.

In tantra this mind state is combined with a great bliss that is produced by bringing the energies (vāyu), into the central channel (dhūtī) of the body. The vāyu is the prana (The Breath) and the dhūtī is the central channel has chakras or cakra which are vital points within the body such as the heart, navel and throat often resembling spokes of a wheel or petals of a lotus. There is a white seminal fluid that resides in the crown during life that can be manipulated to descend through the channels to cause bliss.

This manipulation of the winds in the body is achieved by a variety of methods. The bliss and consciousness attuned on emptiness are united as one. This bliss consciousness is very powerful fast method in achieving the wisdom that understands emptiness.

This bliss consciousness is also transformed through yogic practice into the form of the deity of the tantra.

Method and wisdom in tantra are said to be of one mind. This is not found outside of tantra. In the sutra practices, wisdom is reinforced and boosted by method of practices such as compassion, and method is supported by the wisdom practices of understanding impermanence and the nature of phenomena, but they are never of one entity.

Vajradhara as a tantra form of Buddha is a manifestation of the clear-light mind that we all have. Vajradhara the name of Indra, because 'Vajra' means diamond, as well as the thunderbolt, it is the primordial Buddha which is within each of us. Achieving the 'state of Vajradhara' is synonymous with complete realization.

We all the ability to understand this truth, that there are ways that will lead to liberation and enlightenment. We all have that ability because we all have clear-light minds. So anybody who has that type of revelation or understanding is receiving this from Buddha Vajradhara, because Buddha Vajradhara is not a historical figure from our objective Western point of view of history. Buddha Vajradhara is that within all of us that can be made aware.

In Buddhism, mind is referred to as mental activity. There are many levels of mental activity, and the level of subtly of the mental activity is directly related to the level of subtlety or grossness of the physical basis. So as we die, the consciousness withdraws from having as its basis the grosser aspects of the body which is similar to the process of how we fall asleep.

When mental activity is withdrawing, it it has less and less of a solid basis or foundation which we eventually get down to the clear-light level. Guhyasamaja presents a good amount of detal about reaching this process without dying.

This happens on some level when we sleep, it is similar to dying. We want to simulate this through meditation on the stage of anuttarayoga practice, so that we can actually reach the subtlest level, the clear-light level, without dying. This is also done in shamanism in some traditions, to enter the world of the dead while still alive.

Chapter 17
Chakrasamvara

Chakrasamvara tantra is considered to be of the mother class of the Anuttarayoga Tantra in Vajrayana Buddhism. It is also called the Discourse of Sri Heruka (sriherukabhidhana) and the Samvara Light (Laghusamvara). David B. Gray dates this tantra to the late eight or early ninth century[6].

Tantra is a fast approach to enlightenment. Typically we want things fast because we are impatient, due to laziness. When it comes to enlightenment, we want it as quick as possible so that we can help others. This is fine, tantra is the way, it's not easy, though it's a fast efficient way to reach enlightenment.

In addition to the basics of Buddhism, what Tsongkhapa calls the "three principal pathway minds" (renunciation, bodhichitta, and the correct understanding of voidness) then we need to have confidence in the tantra path and in the anuttarayoga tantra path specifically.

The Cakrasamvara Tantra is mostly dedicated to describing rituals and meditations which produce either mundane siddhis (accomplishment) such as flight or the supramundane siddhi of awakening. These are achieved

---

[6] Gray, David B. The Cakrasamvara Tantra: Its History, Interpretation, and Practice in India and Tibet, Santa Clara University, Religion Compass 1/6 (2007): 695–710

through deity yoga (visualizing oneself as the deity) and the use of mantras.

The central deity of the mandala, Saṃvara, is a form of Heruka, one of the principal yidam or meditational deities of the Sarma schools of Tibetan Buddhism. Heruka is the name of a category of wrathful deities, enlightened beings in Vajrayana Buddhism that adopt a fierce countenance to benefit sentient beings also called Wisdom Kings. They also represent the embodiment of indivisible bliss and emptiness. The Herukas appear as meditational deities for tantric sādhanā (symbolism of union and sexual polarity), usually placed in a mandala and often appearing in Yab-Yum ("father-mother"). It represents the primordial union of wisdom and compassion, depicted as a male deity in union with his female consort. The male figure represents compassion and skillful means, while the female partner represents insight.

Yab-yum is generally understood to represent the primordial (or mystical) union of wisdom and compassion.

In Buddhism the masculine form is active, representing the compassion and skillful means (upaya) that have to be developed in order to reach enlightenment. The feminine form is passive and represents wisdom (prajna), which is also necessary toward enlightenment. When united, they symbolize the union necessary to overcome the veils of Maya, the false duality of object and subject.

In Tibetan Buddhism the same applies with the symbols of the bell and the dorje, which, like the yab-yum, symbolize the dualism that must be exceeded. The dorje in

Sanskrit is Vajra. It is a weapon won in battle which is used as a ritual object to symbolize both the properties of a diamond (indestructibility) and a thunderbolt (irresistible force). It symbolizes the male polarity while the bell symbolizes the female polarity. The Tantric practice leads to rapid development of mind by using the experience of bliss, non-duality, and ecstasy while in communion with one's consort.

Saṃvara as central diety of the mandala. is typically depicted with a blue-coloured body, four faces, and twelve arms, and embracing his consort, the wisdom dakini Vajravārāhī in Yab-Yum. Other forms of the deity are also known with varying numbers of limbs.

Saṃvara and Vajravārāhī are not to be thought of as two different entities, as an ordinary husband and wife are two different people; in reality, their divine embrace is a metaphor for the union of great bliss and emptiness, which are one and the same essence.

Samvara name is often translated to mean "Highest Bliss". Meditation on Cakrasamvara is an advanced practice transmitted by one's lama, and binds the mind of the meditator to enlightenment itself.

Figure 8: Saṃvara with Vajravārāhī in Yab-Yum

Figure 9: Chakrasamvara mandala, Nepalese painting from 1490

The Cakrasamvara Tantra is a relatively short work of about 700 stanzas in 51 chapters. It is a text that is known by several different titles. It refers to itself, at the end of each chapter, as the Discourse of Sri Heruka (sriherukabhidhana). The statement at the end of the text refers to it as the 'Binding of the Wheels', Cakrasamvara; is the name by which it is most commonly known in the Tibetan tradition. In India, it was commonly called 'Samvara Light', Laghusamvara.

It is a rather cryptic text, focusing on elements of practice, and doesn't give sufficient information for one to actually practice. This is common of esoteric Buddhist literature, and was almost certainly intentional.

Scriptures such as the Cakrasamvara Tantra were not meant to provide a full interpreting of the tradition's practices, but merely hint at these, as the 'secret' to be attained only by those initiated by a master. Only then would the master disclose the full details of practice to the initiated adept.

The Cakrasamvara Tantra is a short but fascinating work. It is a text largely focused on ritual, which was composed outside of the mainstream Indian Buddhist monastic centers, with significant dependence on Saiva Hindu sources. In spite of its unorthodox origin, it became, by the tenth century, the focus of one of the most important Indian tantric Buddhist practice traditions.

This was the beginning of the 'second transmission' of the dharma to Tibet. This ensured its successful transmission to Tibet and its continued practice in Tibetan Buddhist communities around the world.

Summary

In this book I have explained about the three blind worlds of the ten worlds of Buddhism. Ksitigarbha who is a Bodhisattva name can be translated as "Earth Treasury"as one who instruct all beings in the six lower realms, he shines the light in the first three blind realms, Hell, hungry ghosts and animal. As we learn to look within and accept that we are a human animal that is no better than those who walk on all four, we can be free of the shame and guilt from social indoctrination that caused the split between conscious and subconscious that oppressed us by shaming us for being human. Society has put this image out there of what is considered the perfect or idea person. It's usually a false image that's impossible to live up to; so many people feel shame when they fail to love up to that image. Getting rid of self-hatred and being whole by uniting all parts of us, our strengths and weakness, then we are in the step of Liberation (Enlightenment).

As "Earth Treasury" there within the earth (within us) you will find treasures just like you would in the actual earth. Even in Greek myth, the underworld is called Hades and the Latinized form of Greek Πλουτων (Plouton), derived from πλουτος (ploutos) meaning "wealth", is where we get the word Pluto.

This is the same symbolism that within the dark places within us is a treasure of wealth that we will find,

Ksitigarbha has a halo and carries the wish-fulfilling jewel that is a luminous pearl to light up the darkness.

When we follow the path, we are Ksitigarbha, the one who lights the darkness.

Bibliography

The Tibetan Book of the Dead, **ISBN-10:** 1570627479 also called Bardo Thodol which means Liberation Through Hearing During the Intermediate State emphasizes the practical advice that the book offers to the living. The insightful commentary by Chögyam Trungpa. The Profound Dharma of Self-Liberation through the Intention of the Peaceful and Wrathful Ones, revealed by Karma Lingpa (1326–1386).

A Lamp to Illuminate the Five Stages: Teachings on Guhyasamāja Tantra by Tsongkhapa, **ISBN-10:** 0861714547 is a comprehensive presentation of the highest yoga class of Buddhist tantra, especially the key practices - the so-called five stages (pancakrama) - of the advanced phase of Guhyasamaja tantra. Beginning with a thorough examination of the Indian sources, Tsongkhapa draws particularly from the writings of Nagarjuna, Aryadeva, Candrakirti, and Naropa to develop a definitive understanding of the Vajrayana completion stage.

The Small Book: A Revolutionary Alternative for Overcoming Alcohol and Drug Dependence by Jack Trimpey **ISBN**-10: 1522663851 Offering an alternative to twelve-step programs, a supportive guide explains how to identify the impulse to use intoxicants, learn self-control, value sobriety, and replace addiction with self-supportive behaviors. The Doctrine of Variable Human Worth, Again The real culprit in the roller coaster ride, the idea that seems to make it impossible to get off and just enjoy life for what it is, is the Doctrine of Variable Human Worth. You will recall from Chapter 8 how this doctrine was the wedge driven between love and self.

https://en.wikipedia.org/wiki/Naraka_(Buddhism)

https://suttacentral.net/en/an3.36

https://studybuddhism.com/en/advanced-studies/vajrayana/tantra-advanced/what-is-vajrabhairava-yamantaka-practice

https://www.huffingtonpost.com/kamlesh-d-patel/yama-the-five-vows-of-the_b_13276536.html

http://www.seanfeitoakes.com/yama-and-mara-hindu-and-buddhist-personifications-of-death-a-hypothesis/

http://www.bodhicitta.net/The%20Wheel%20of%20Sharp%20Weapons.htm